GRAPES
COLORING BOOK

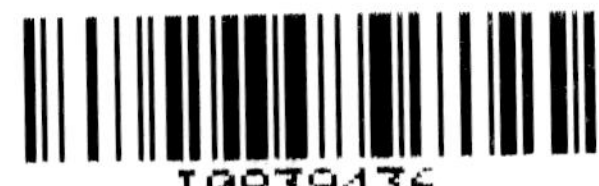

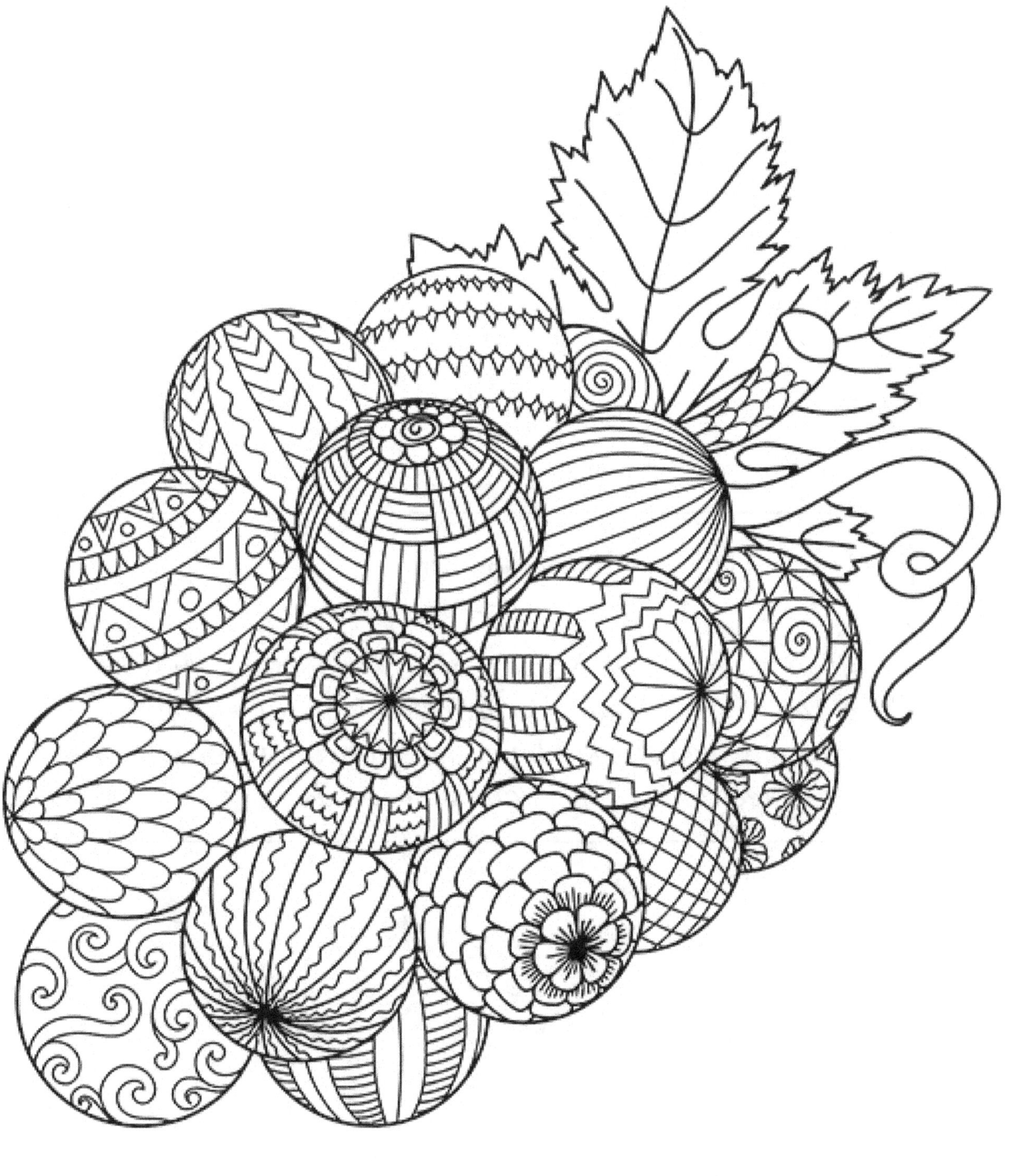

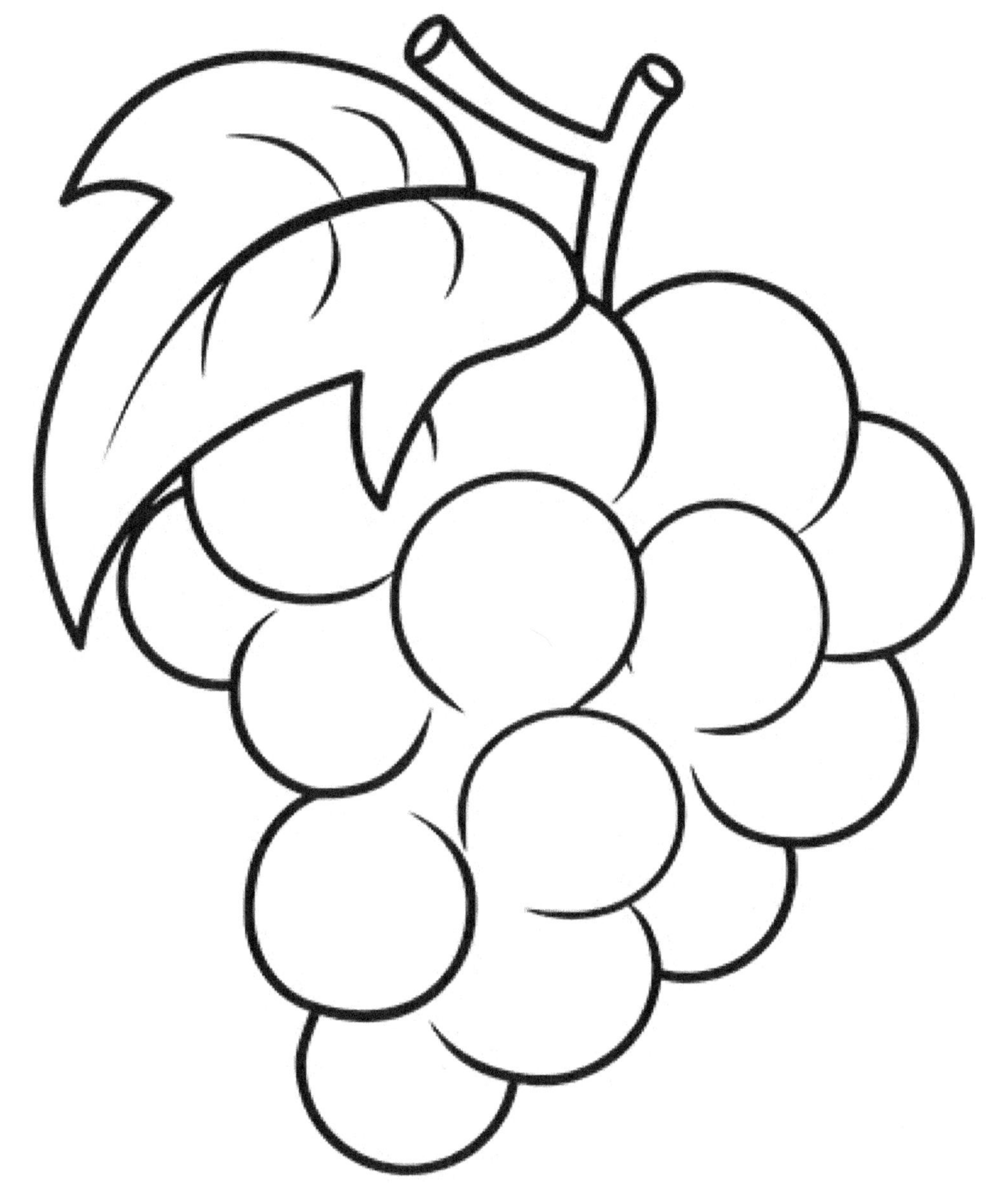

This Coloring book Belongs to:

Color test Page

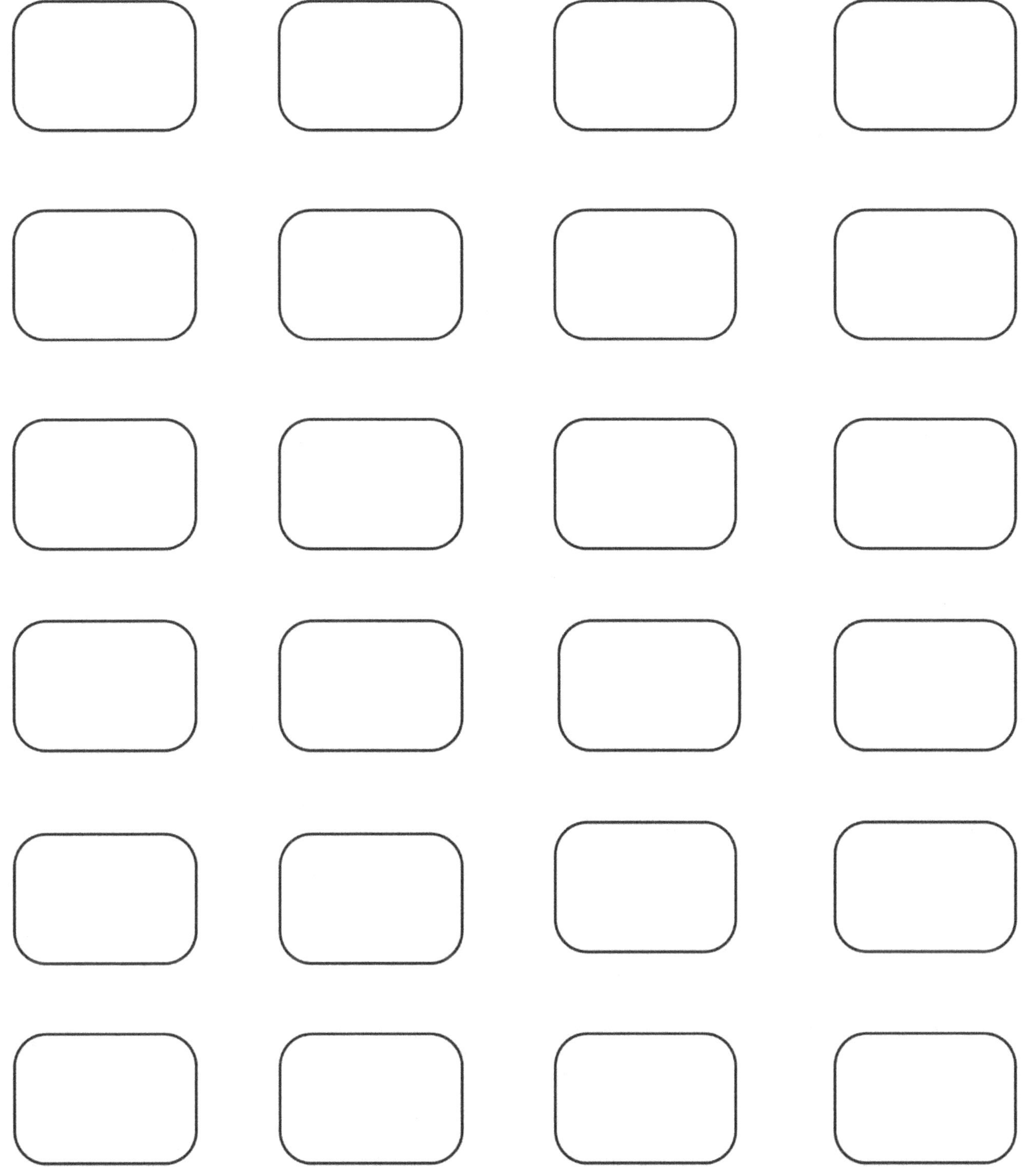

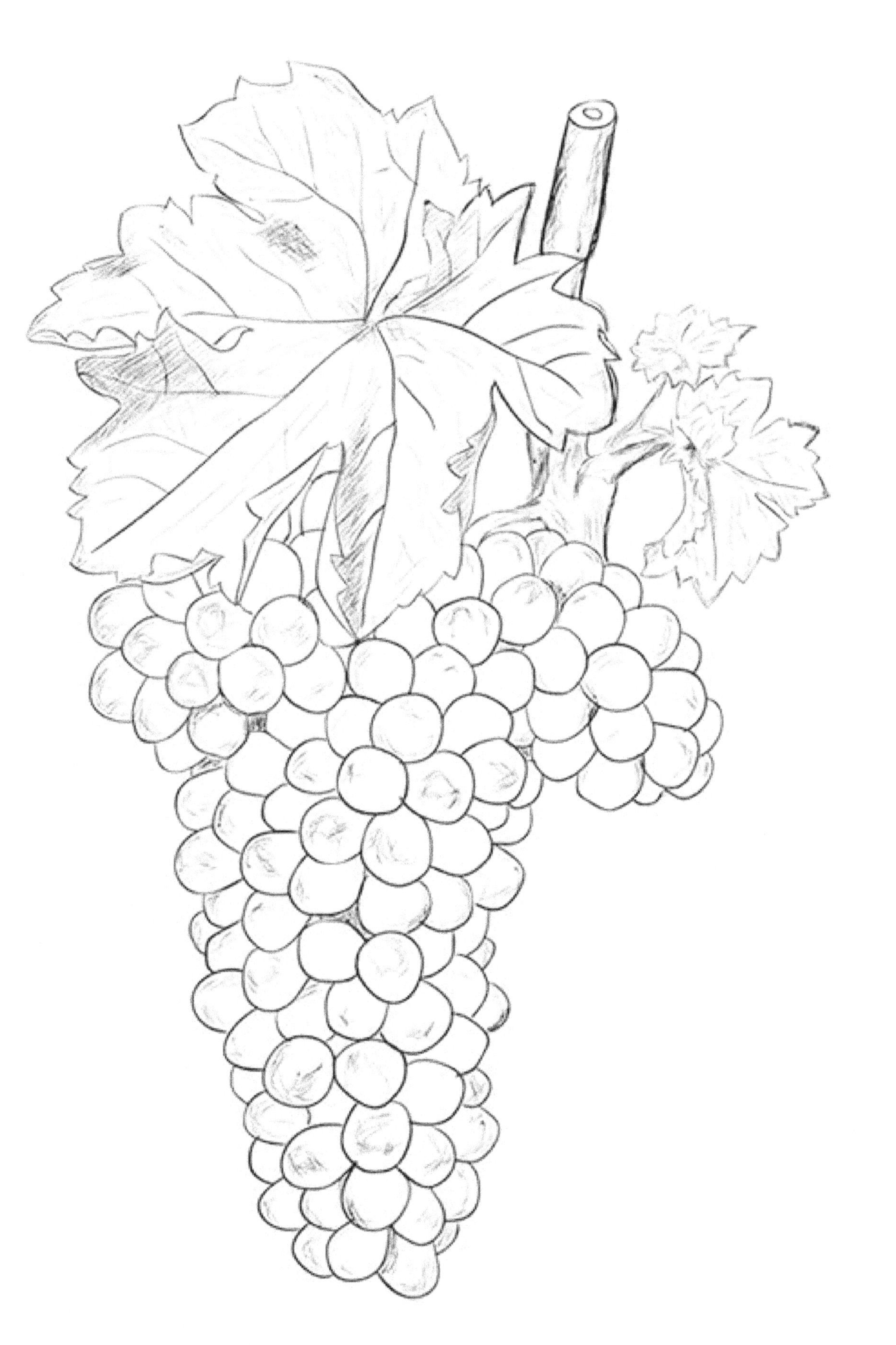

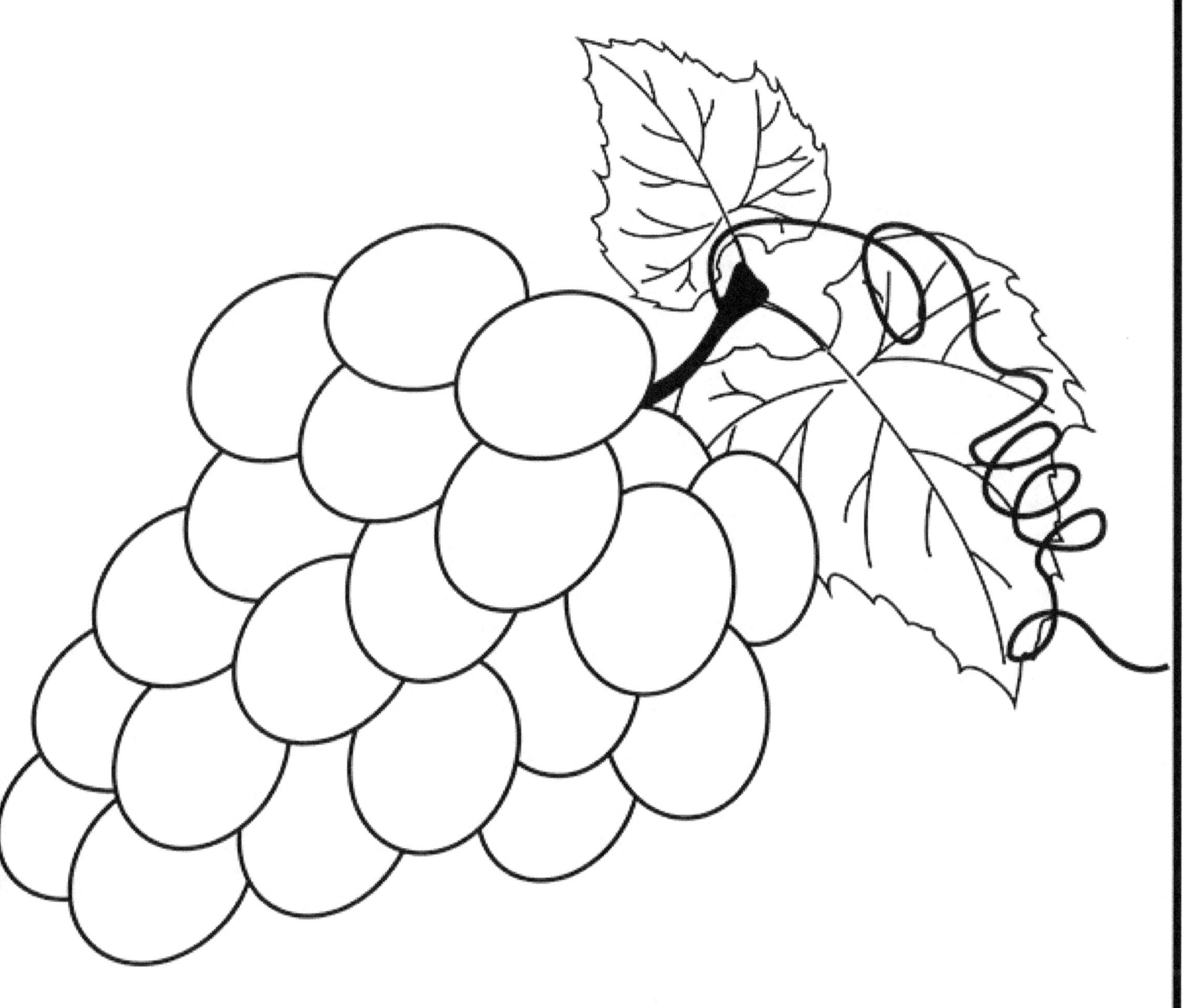

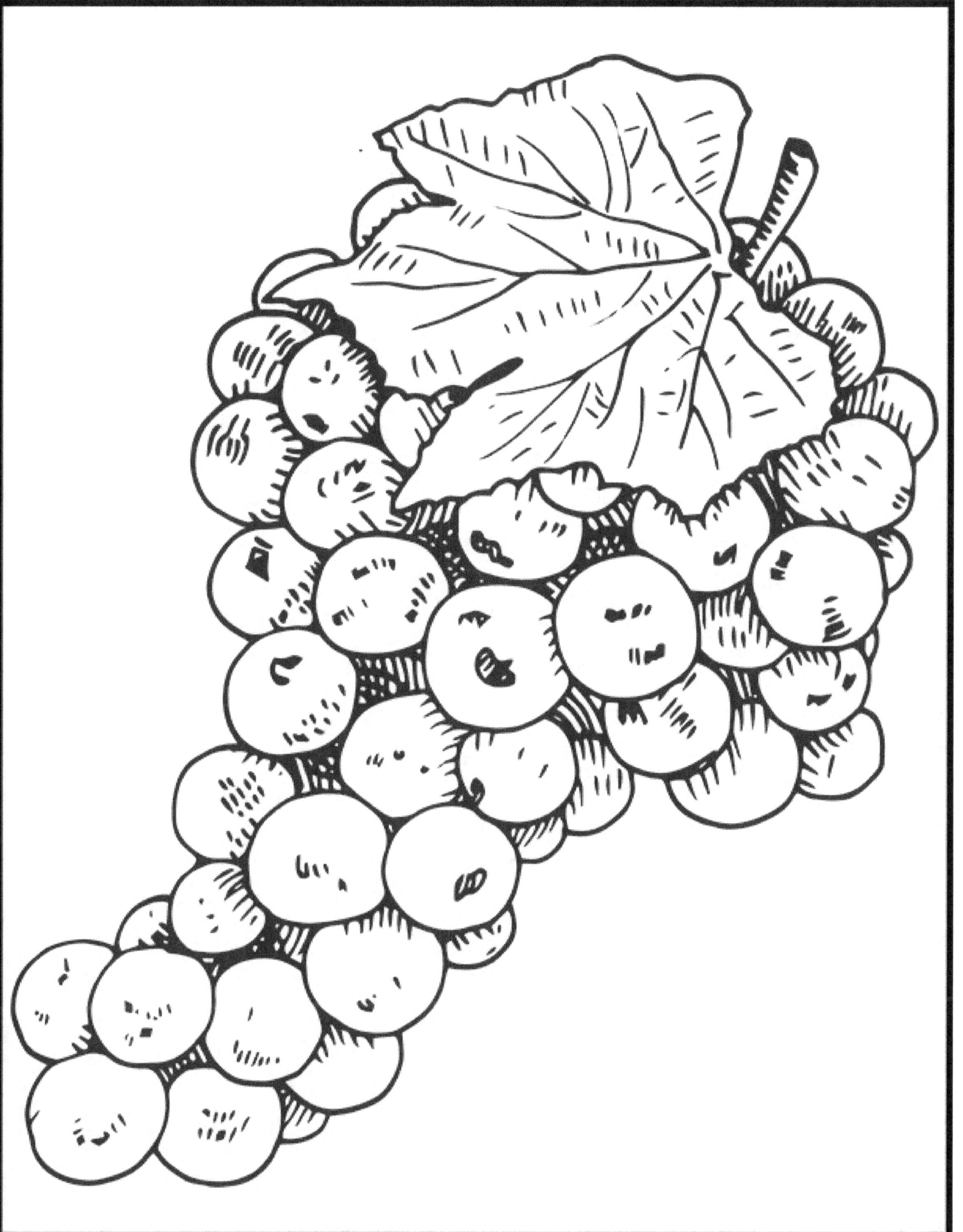

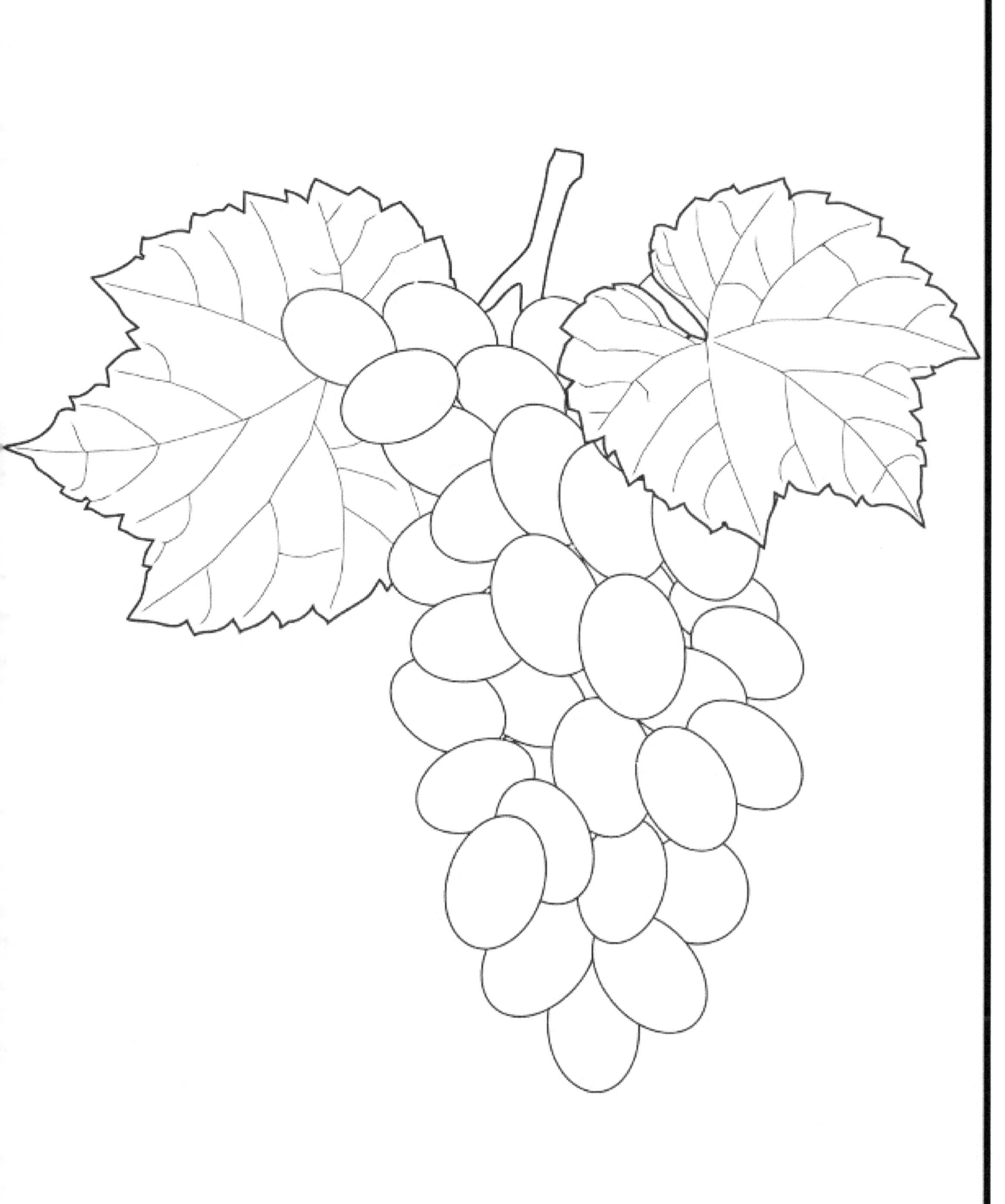

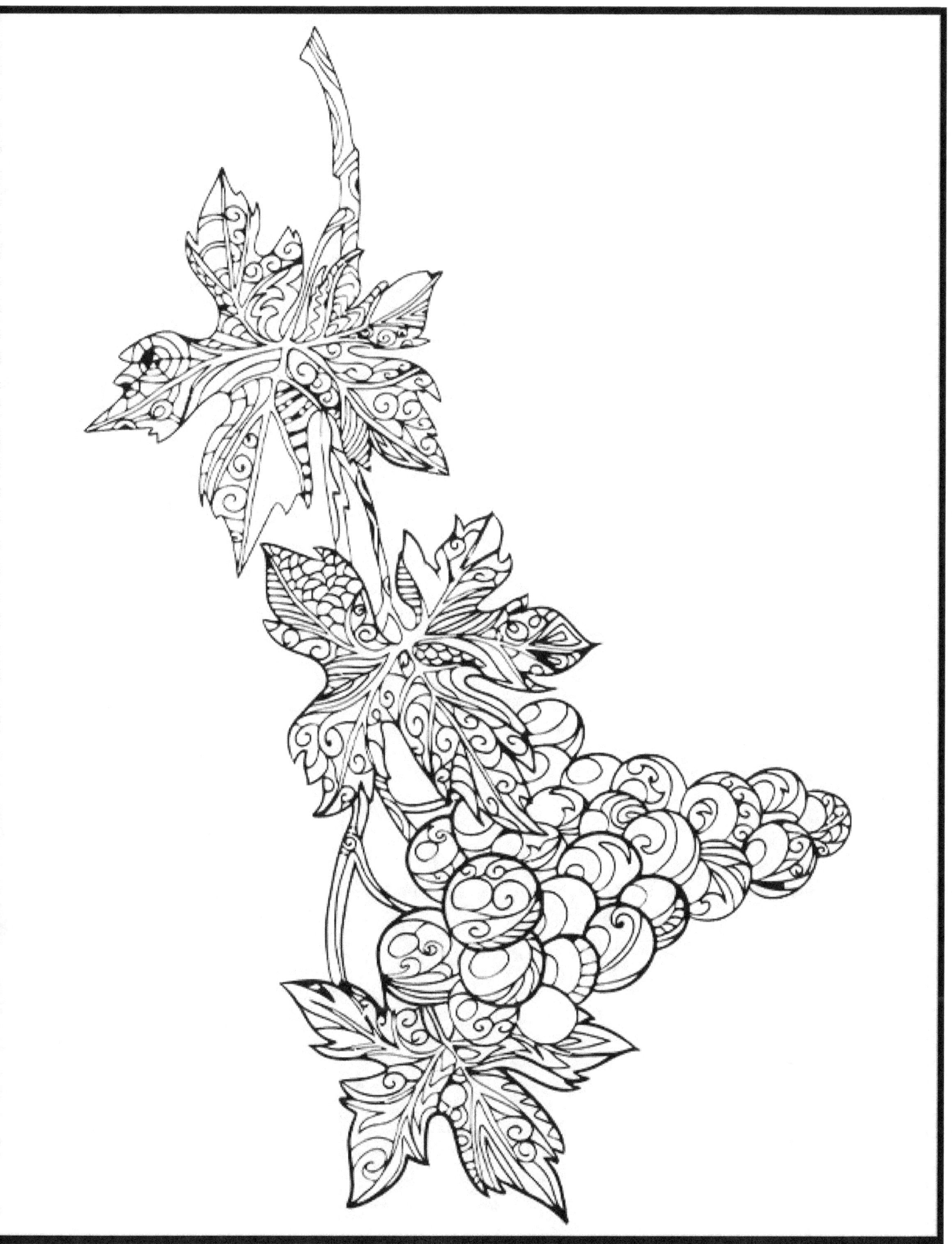

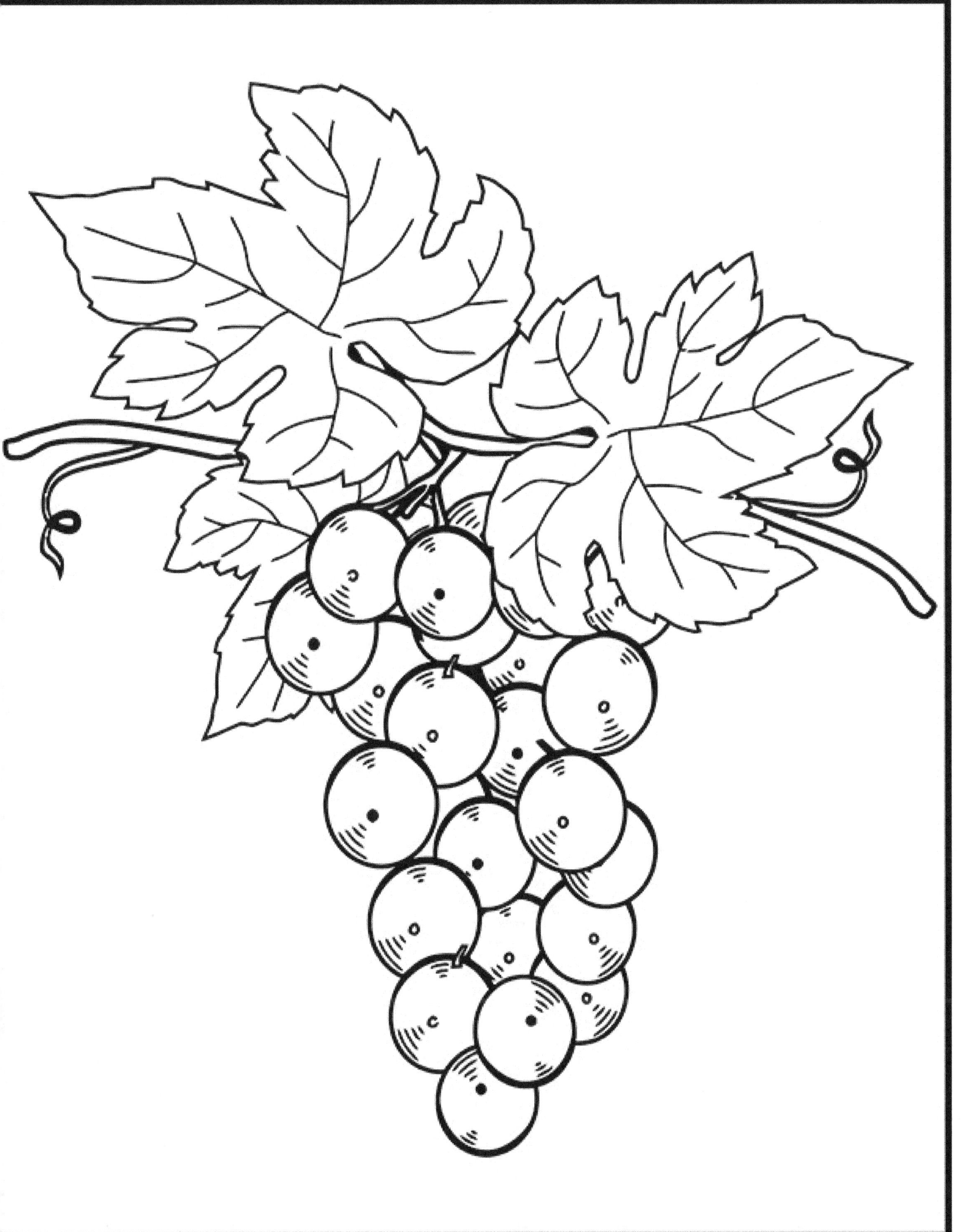

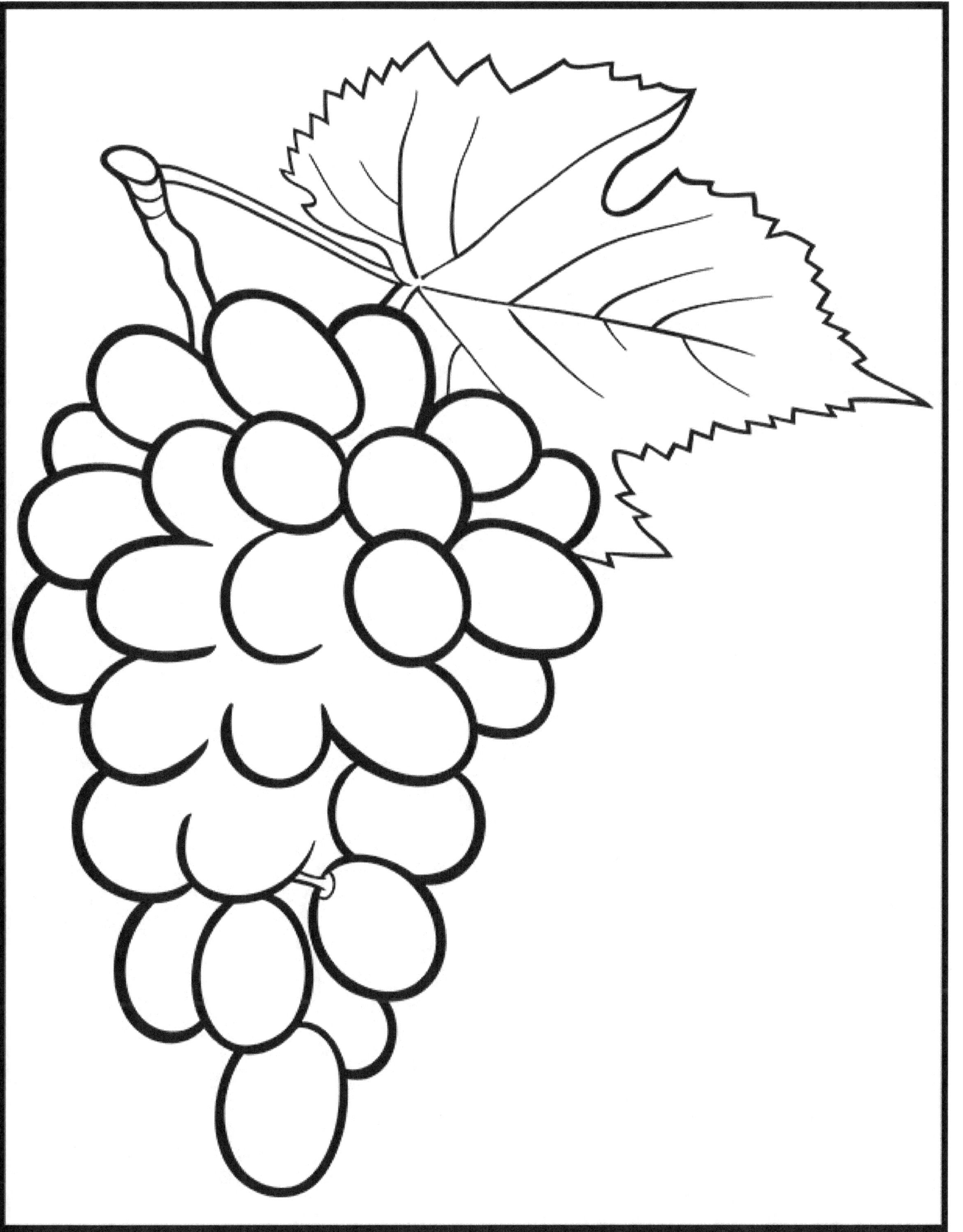

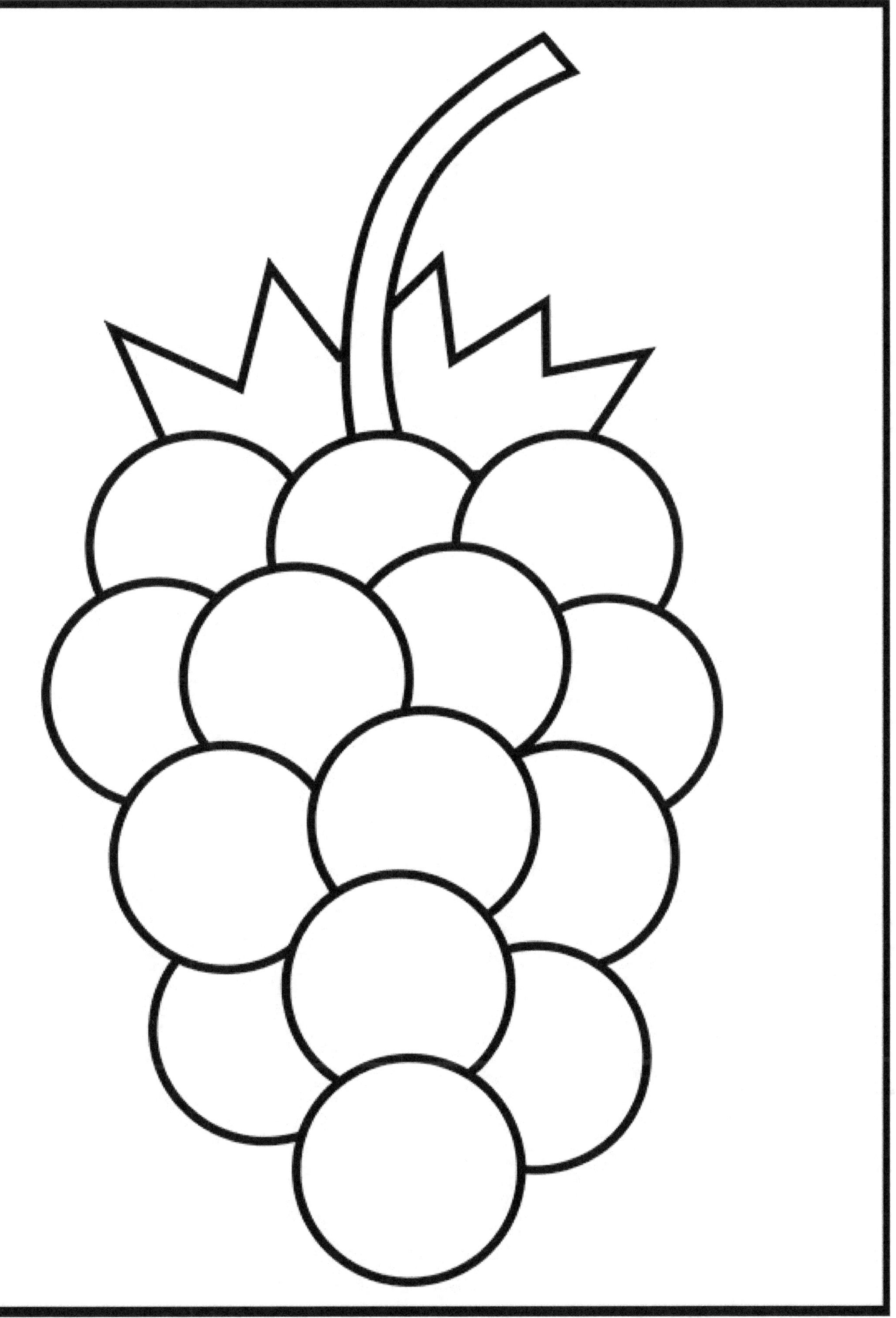

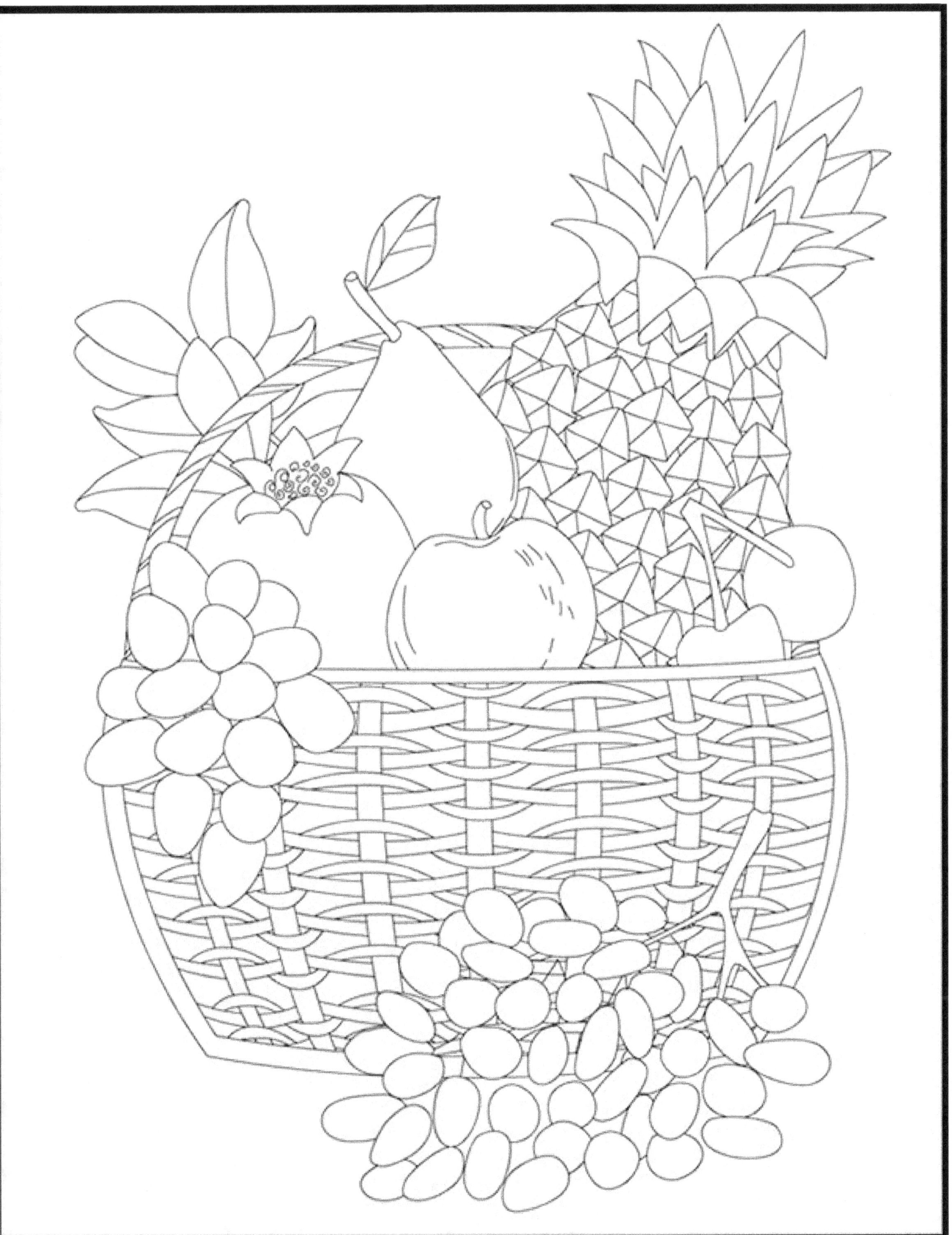

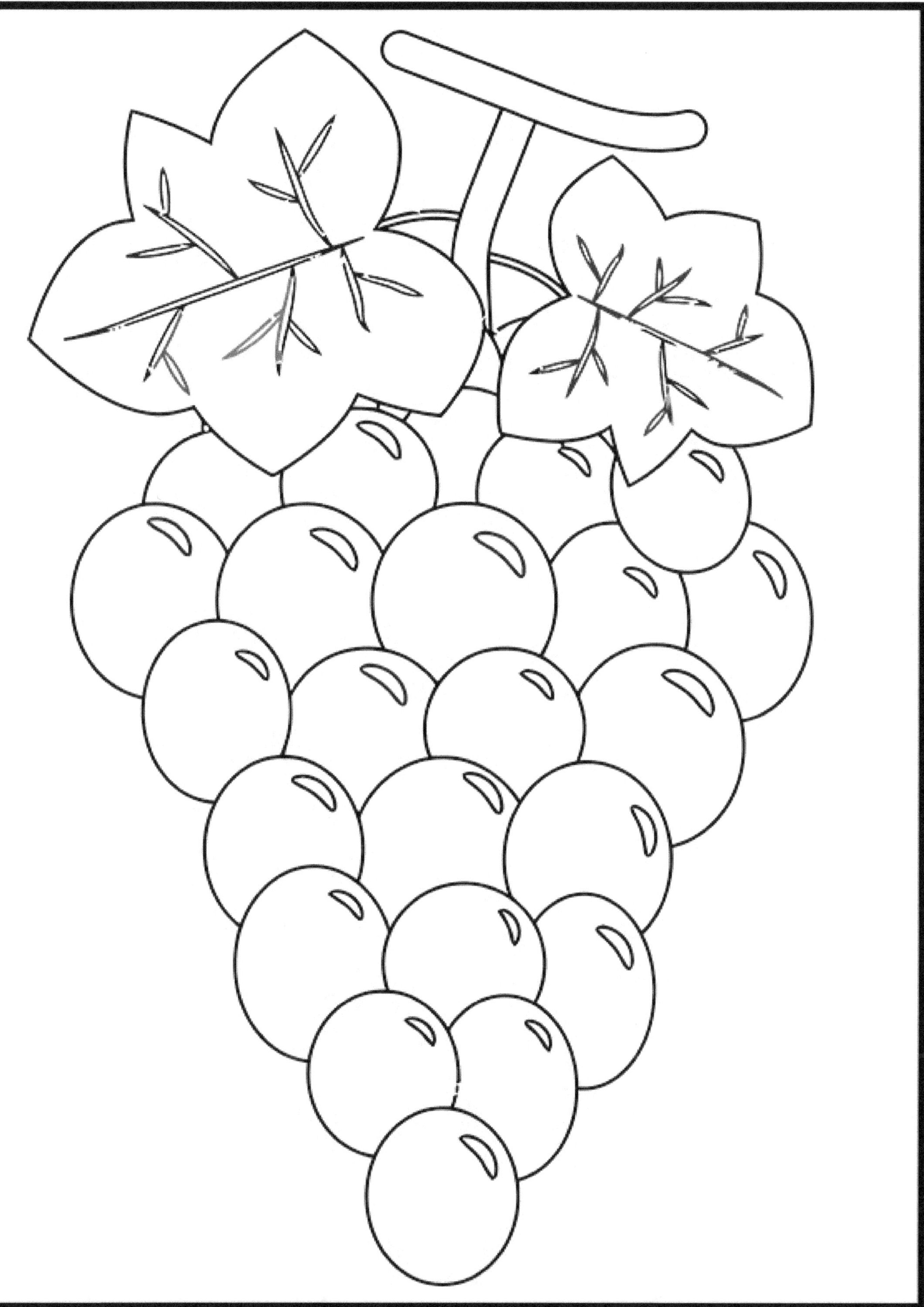

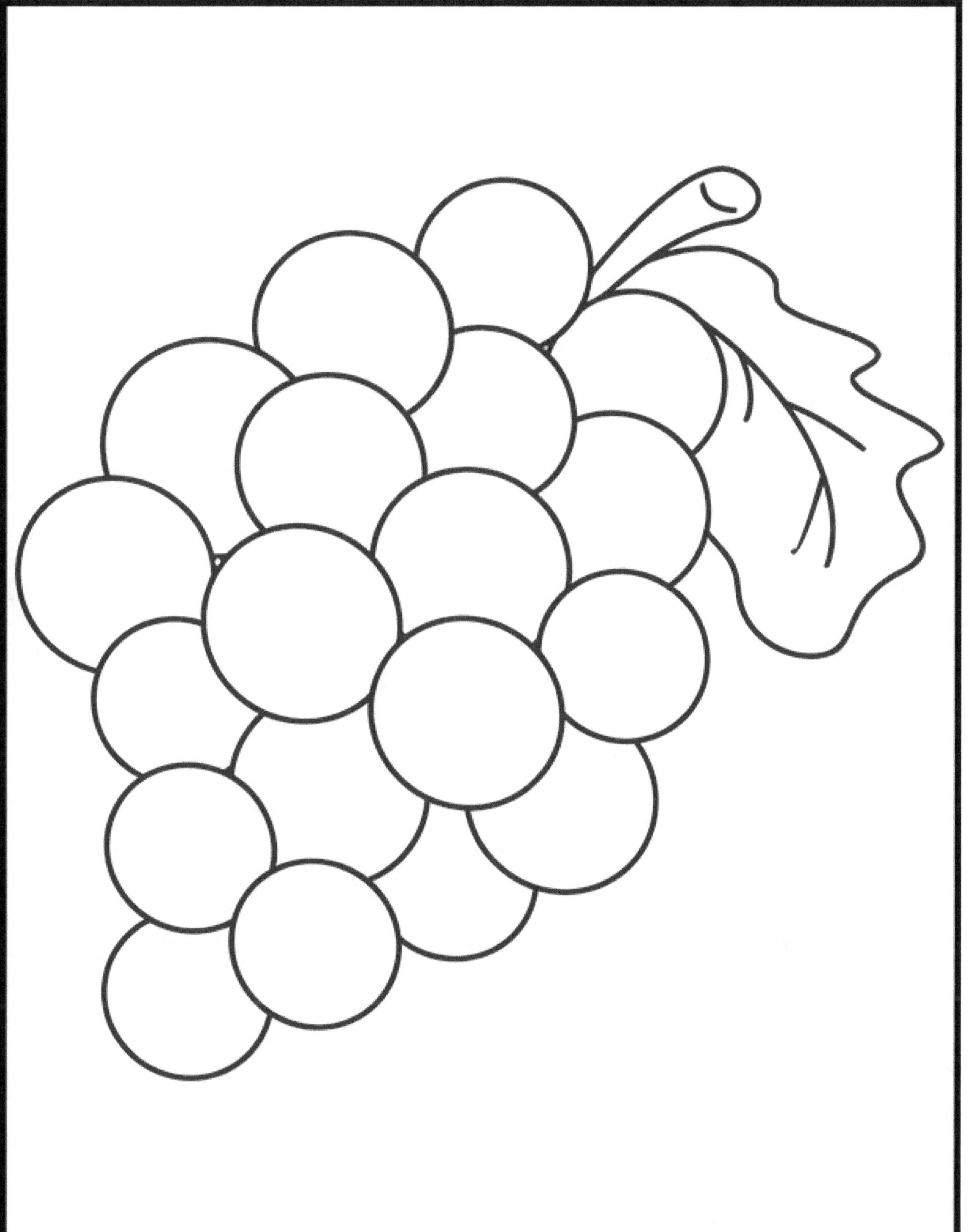

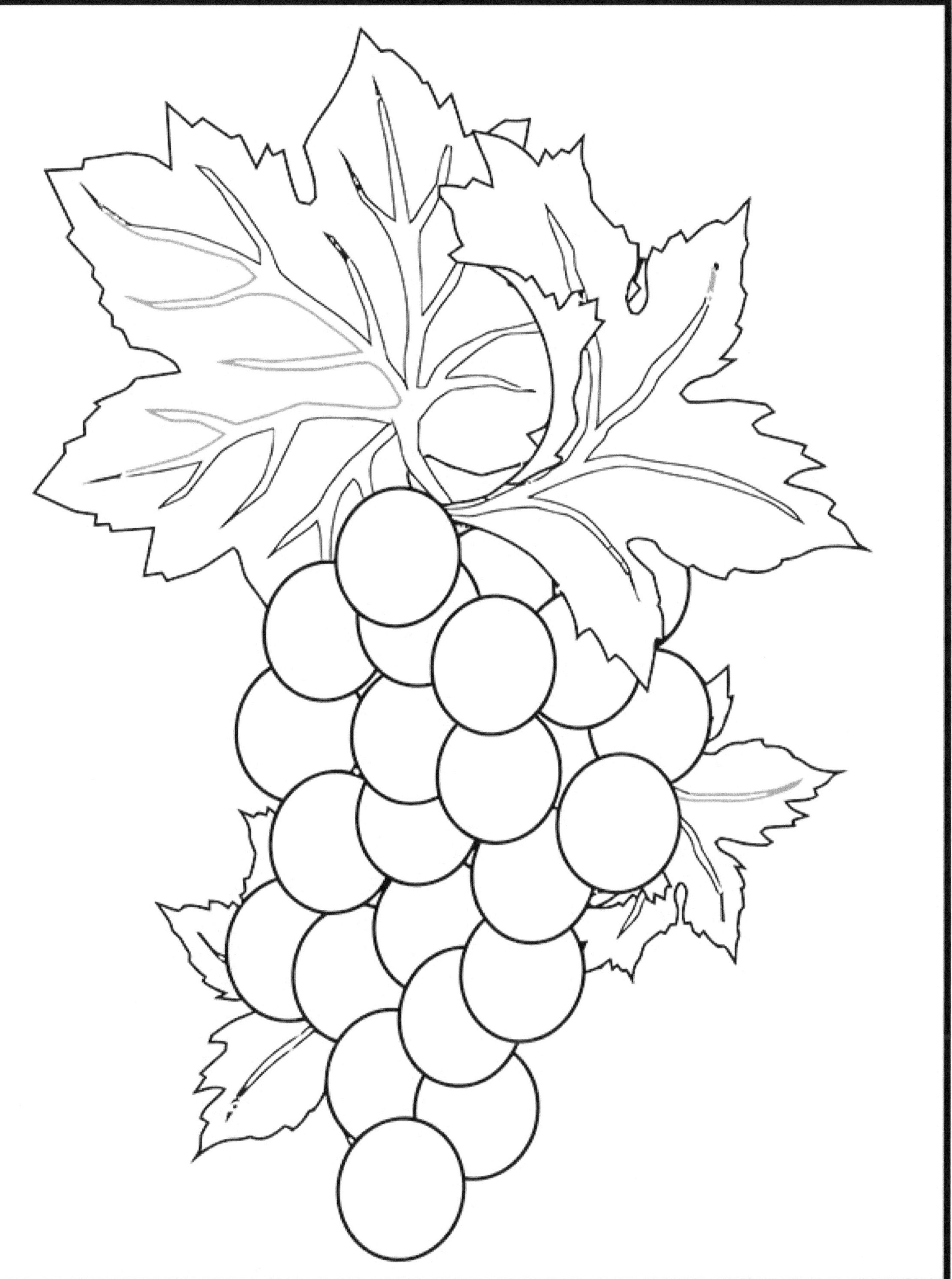

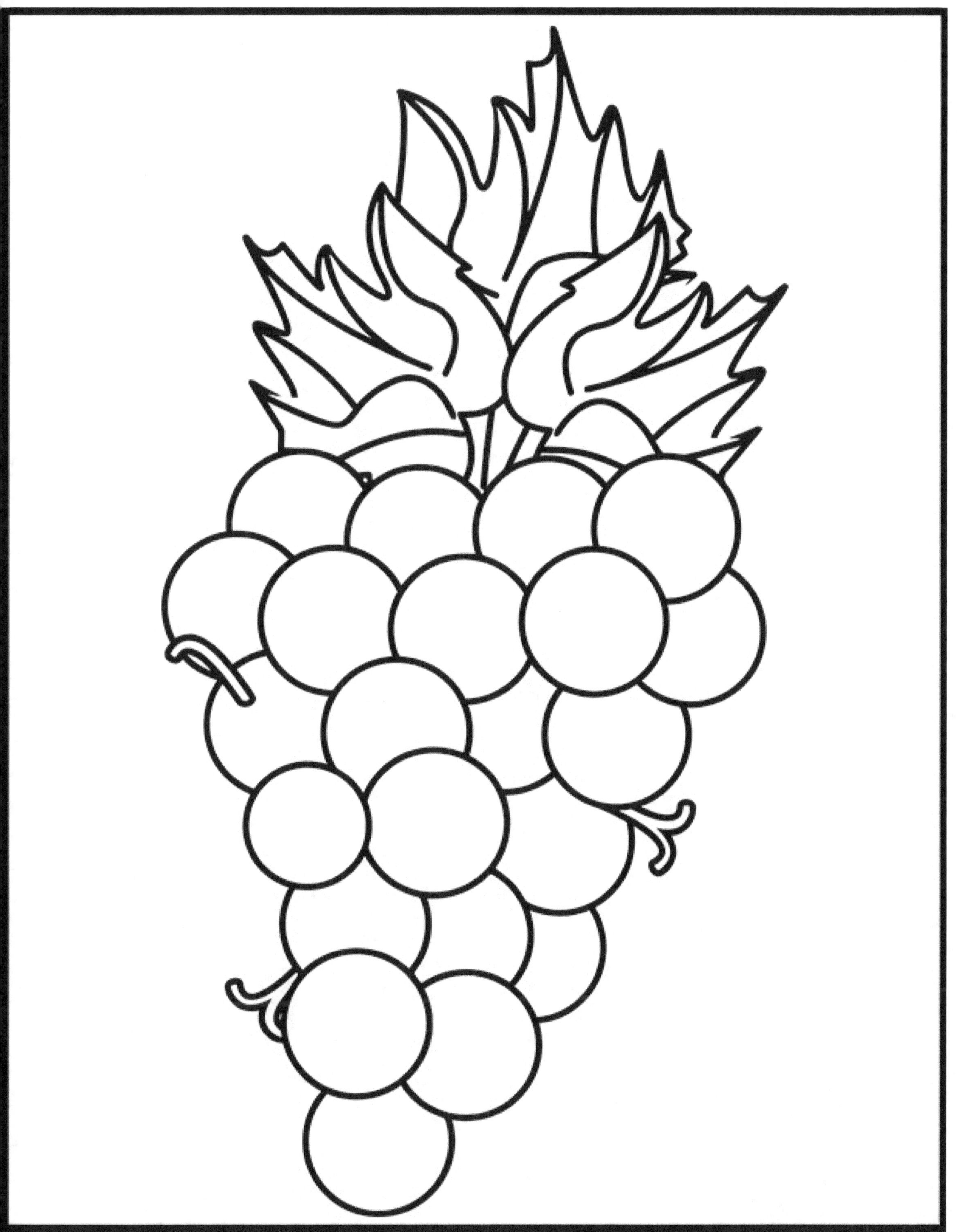

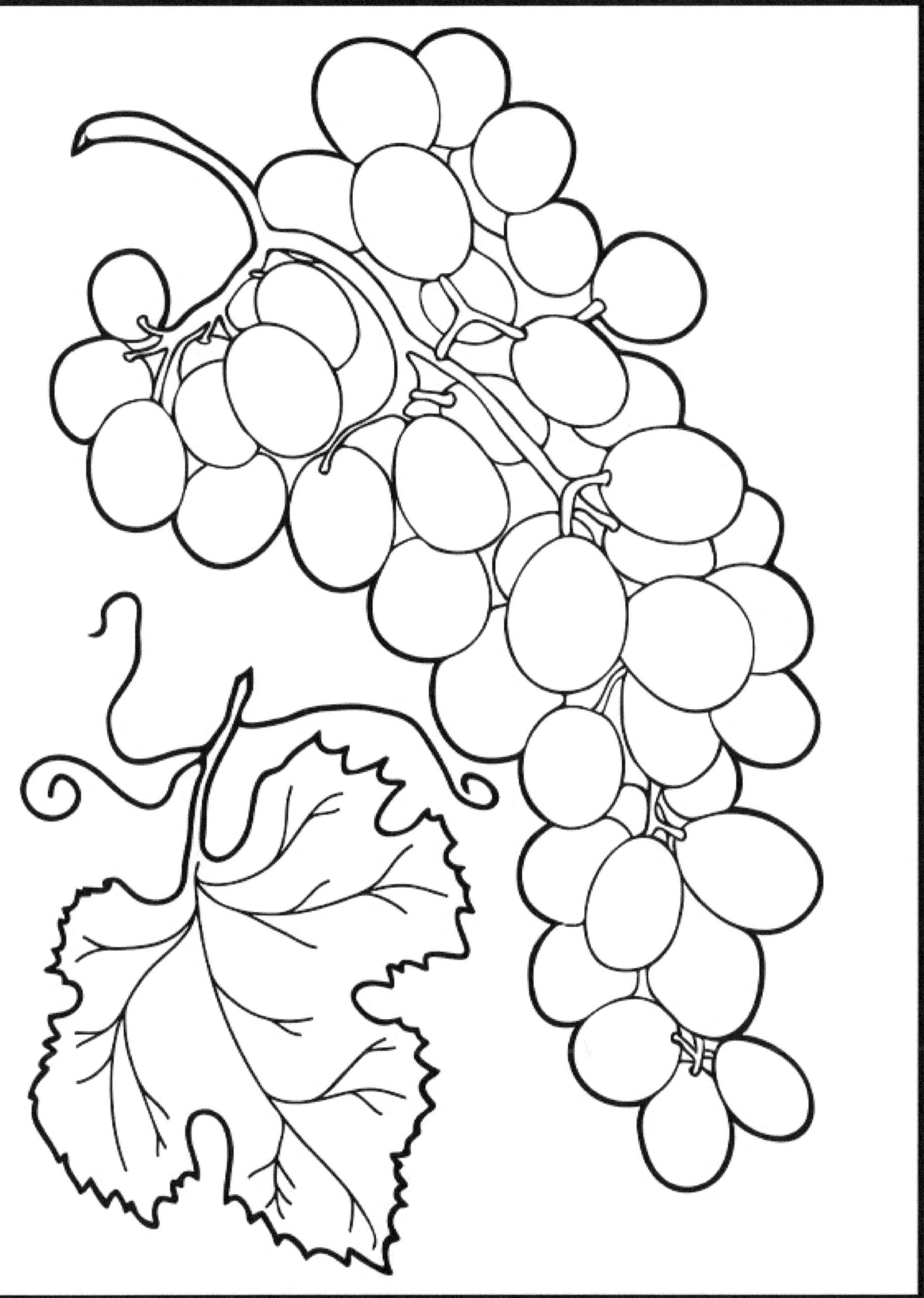

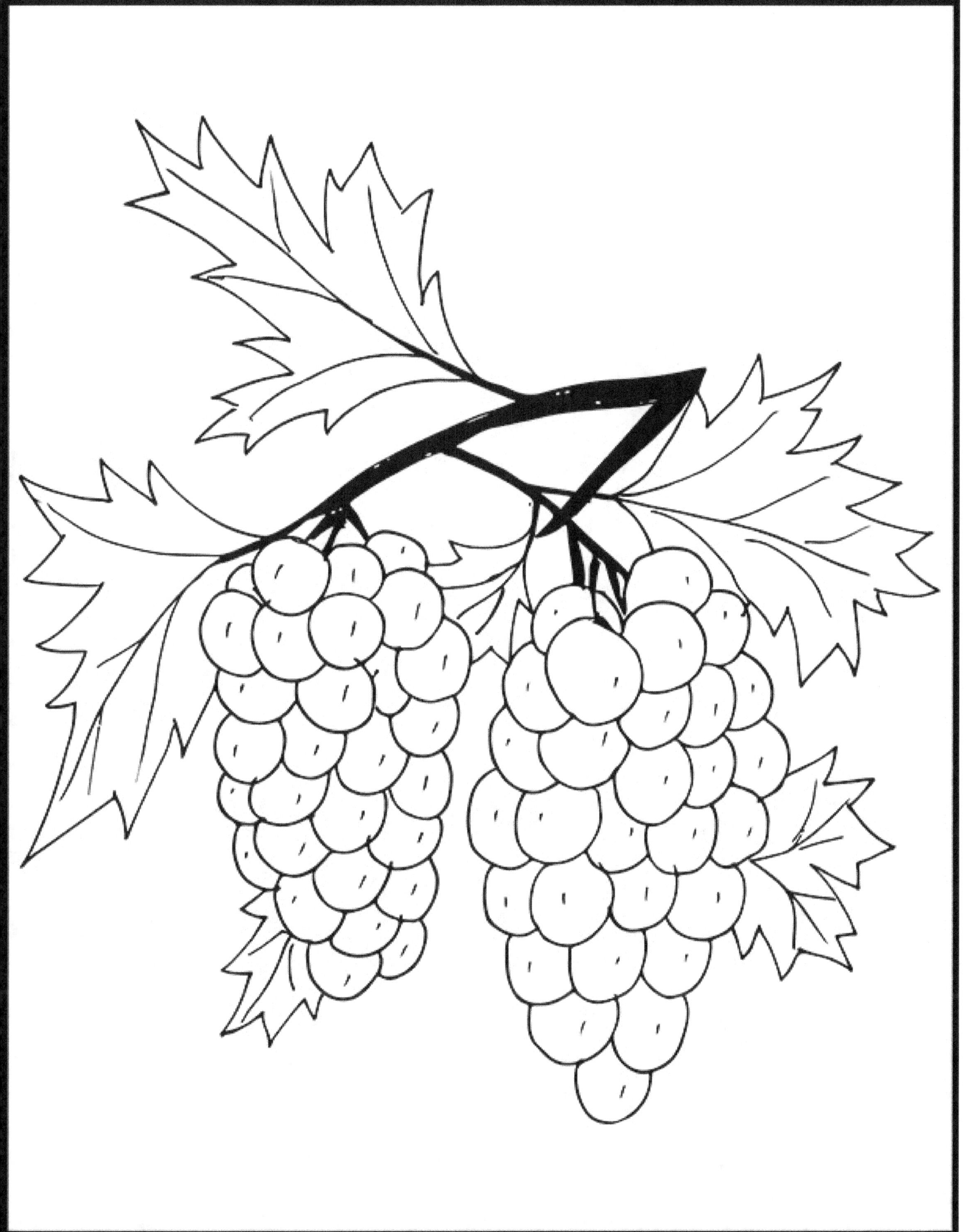

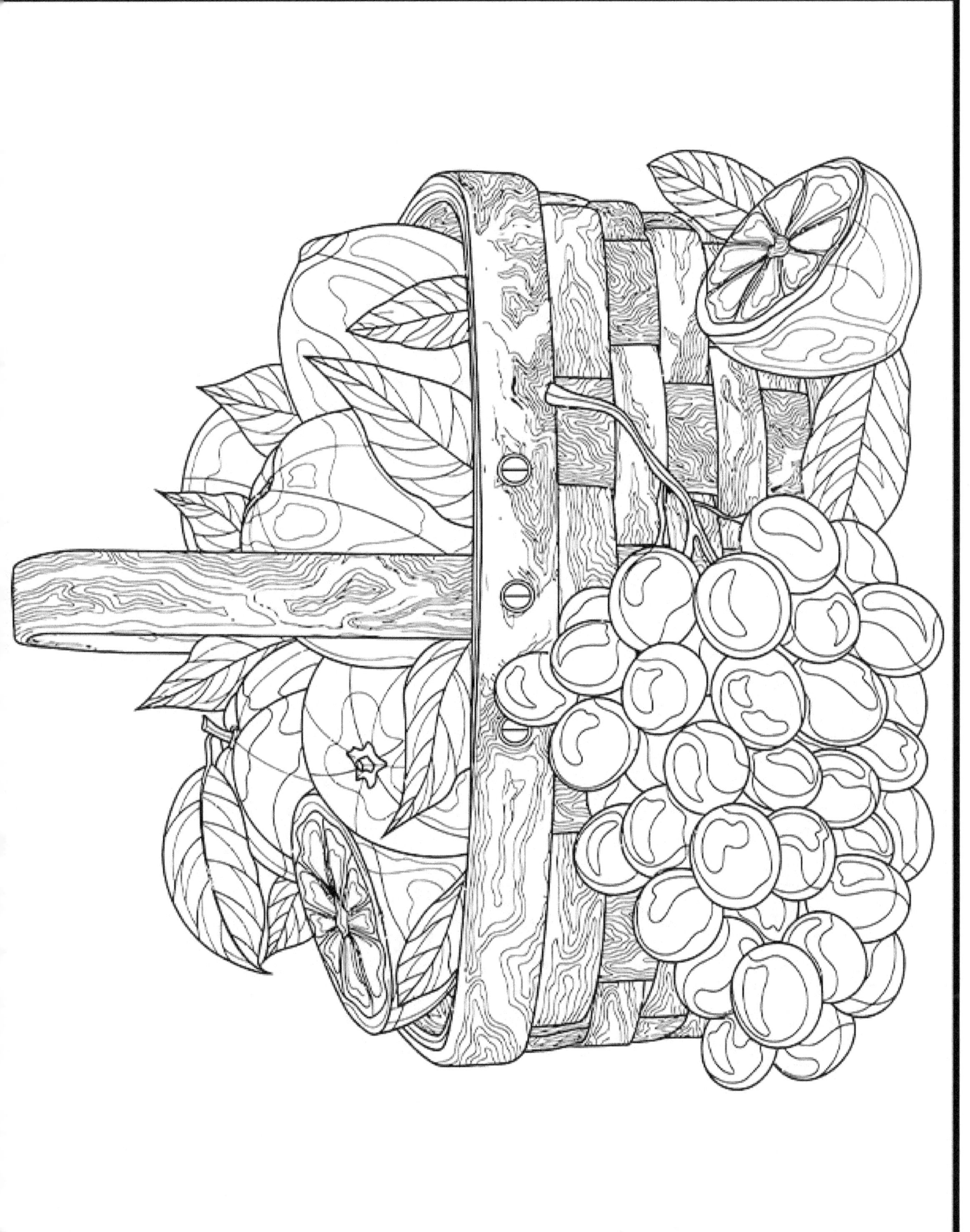

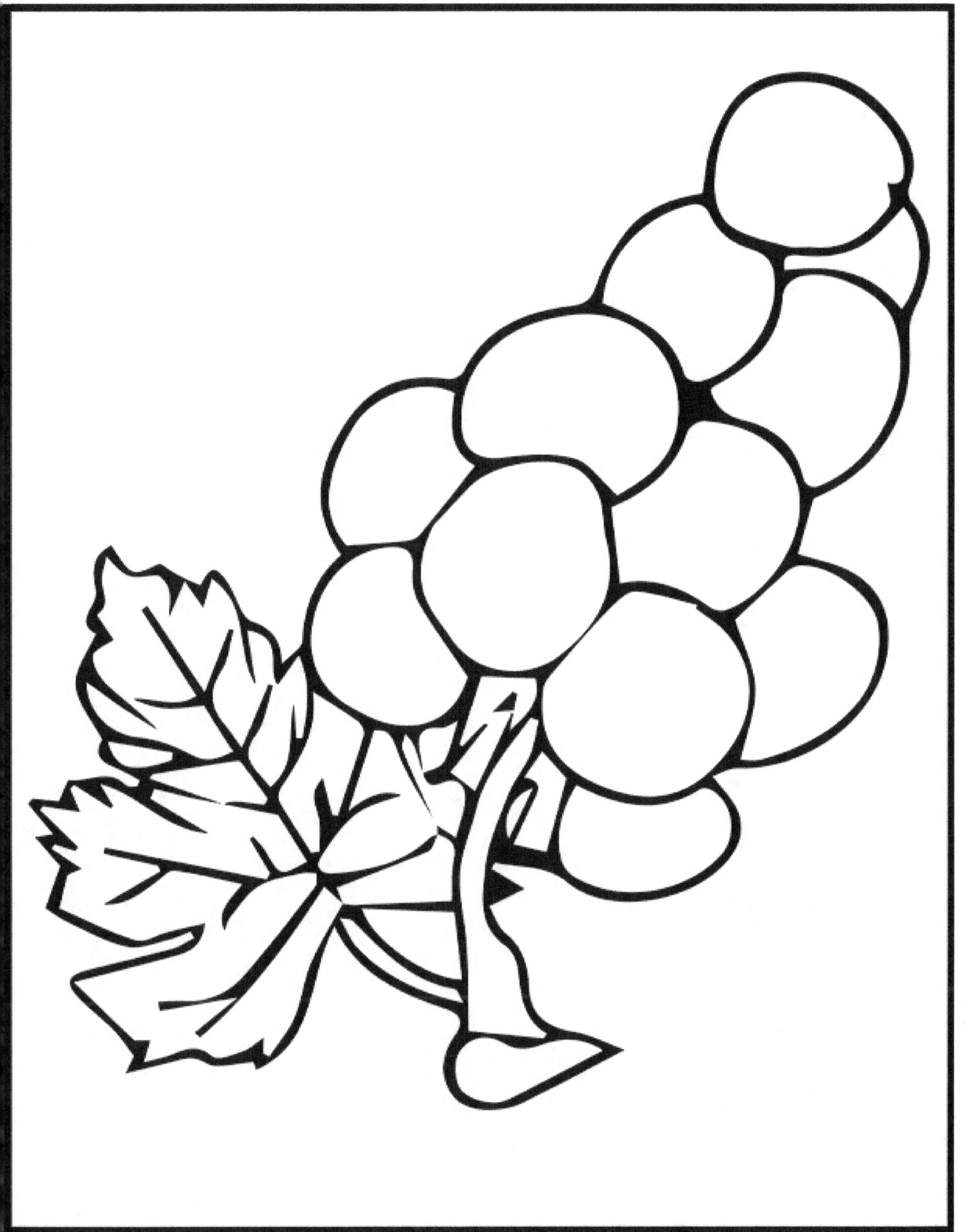

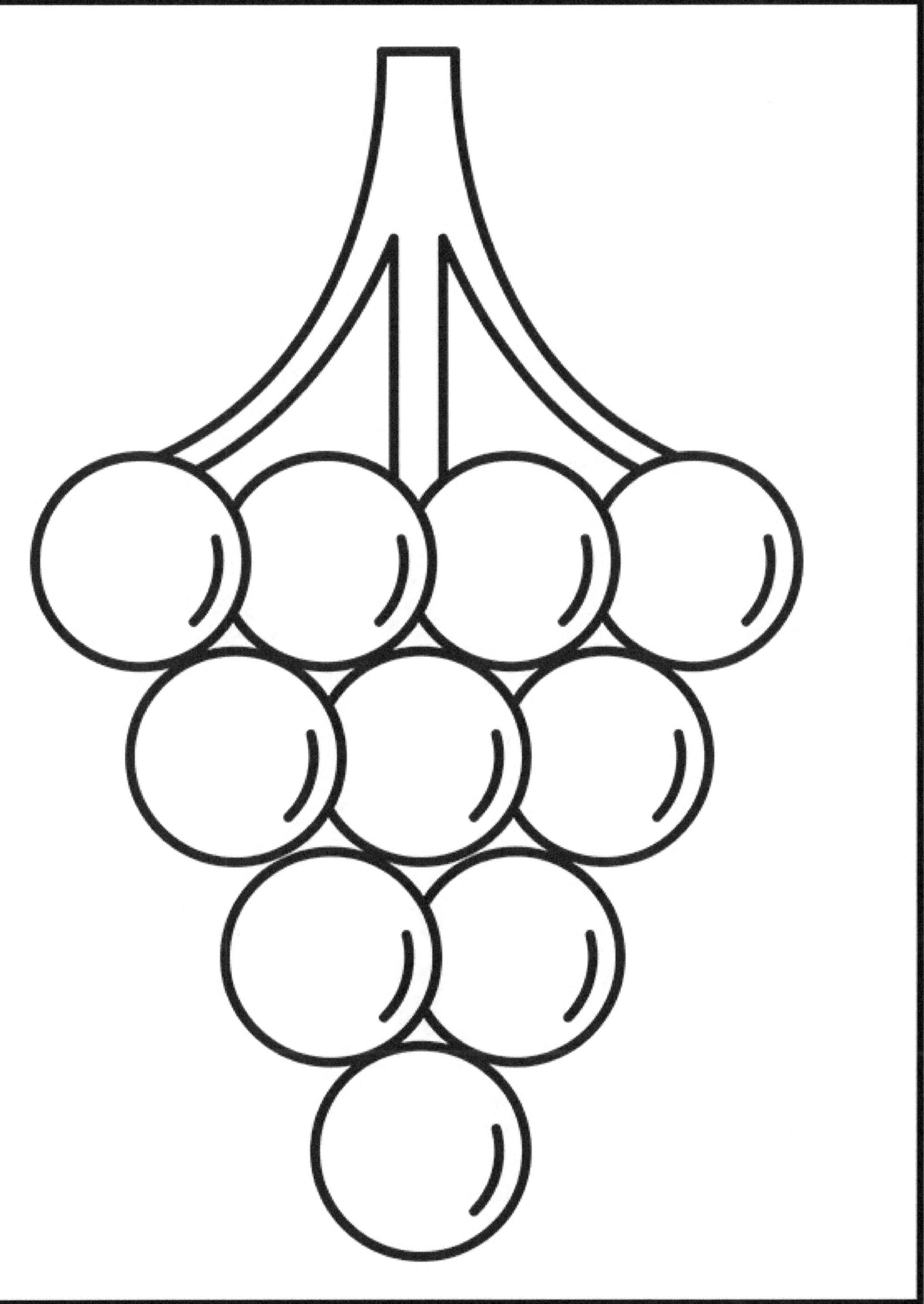

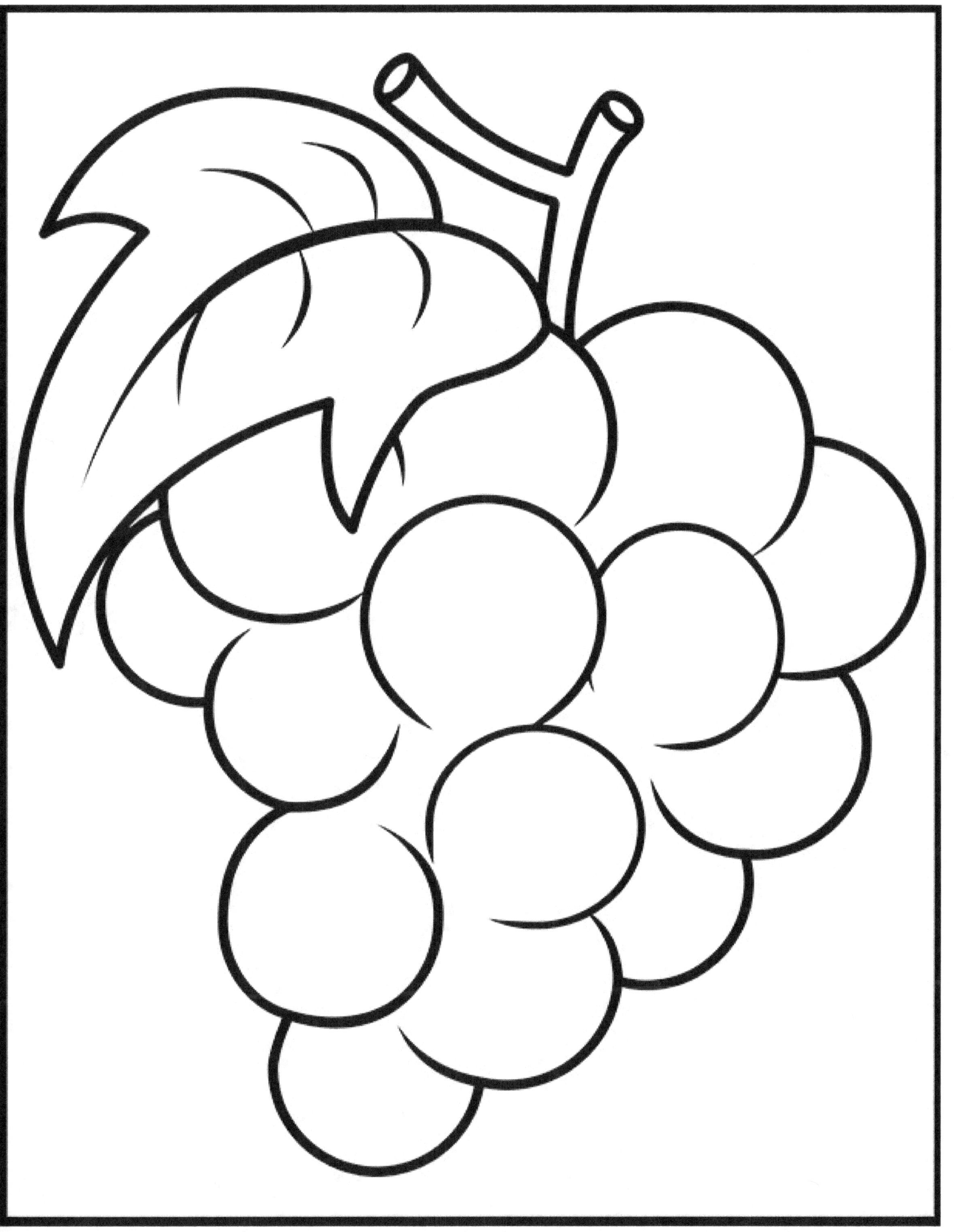

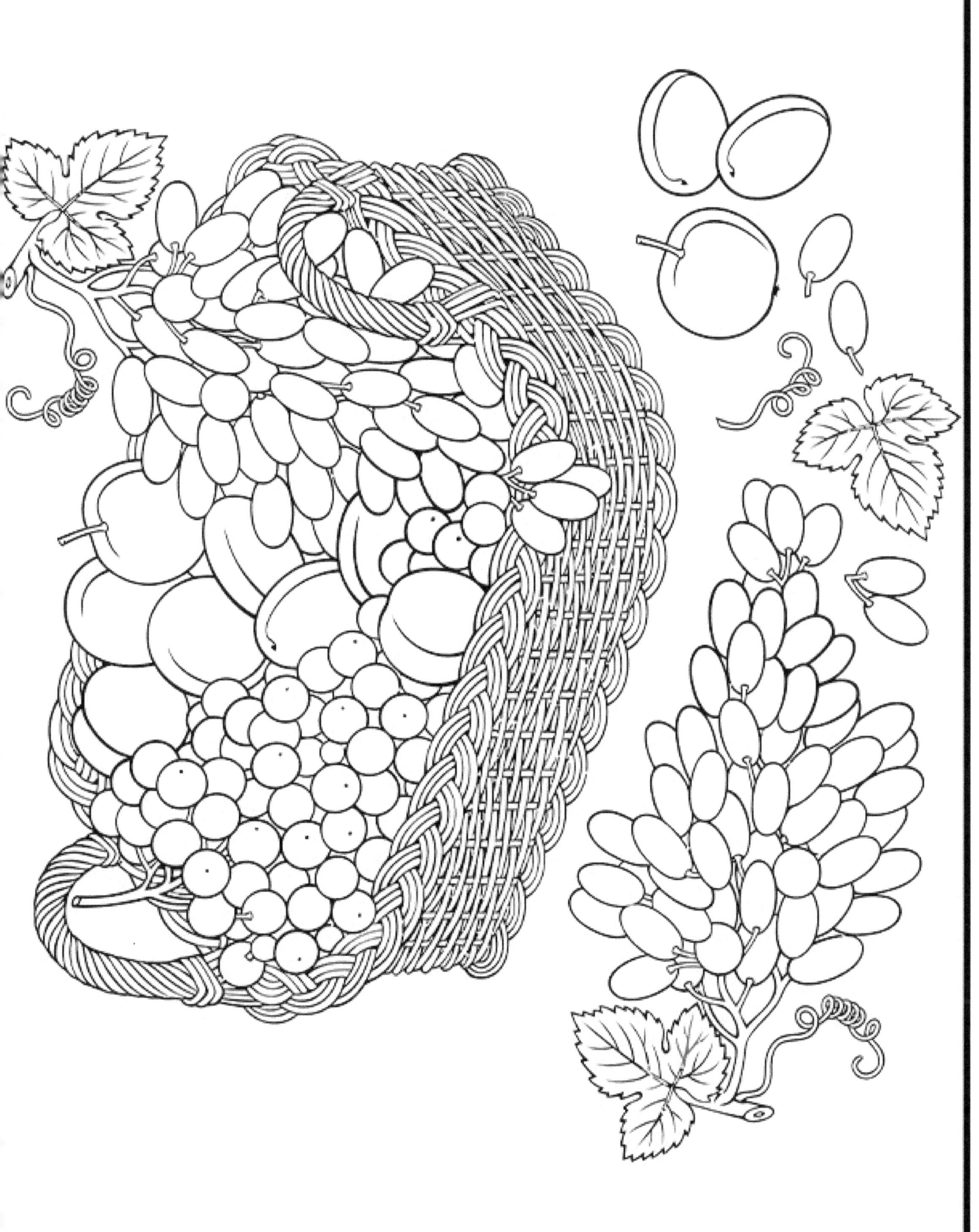

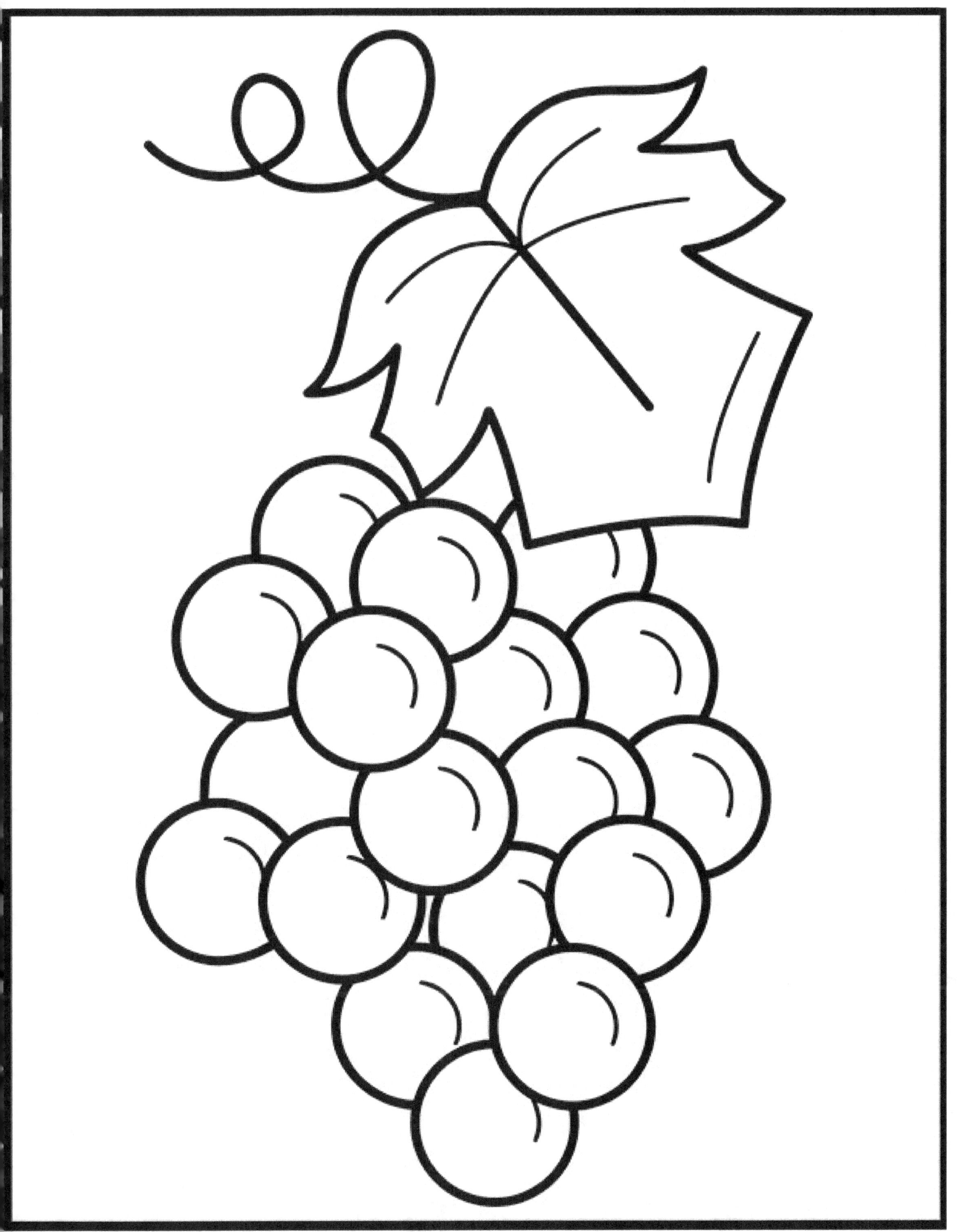

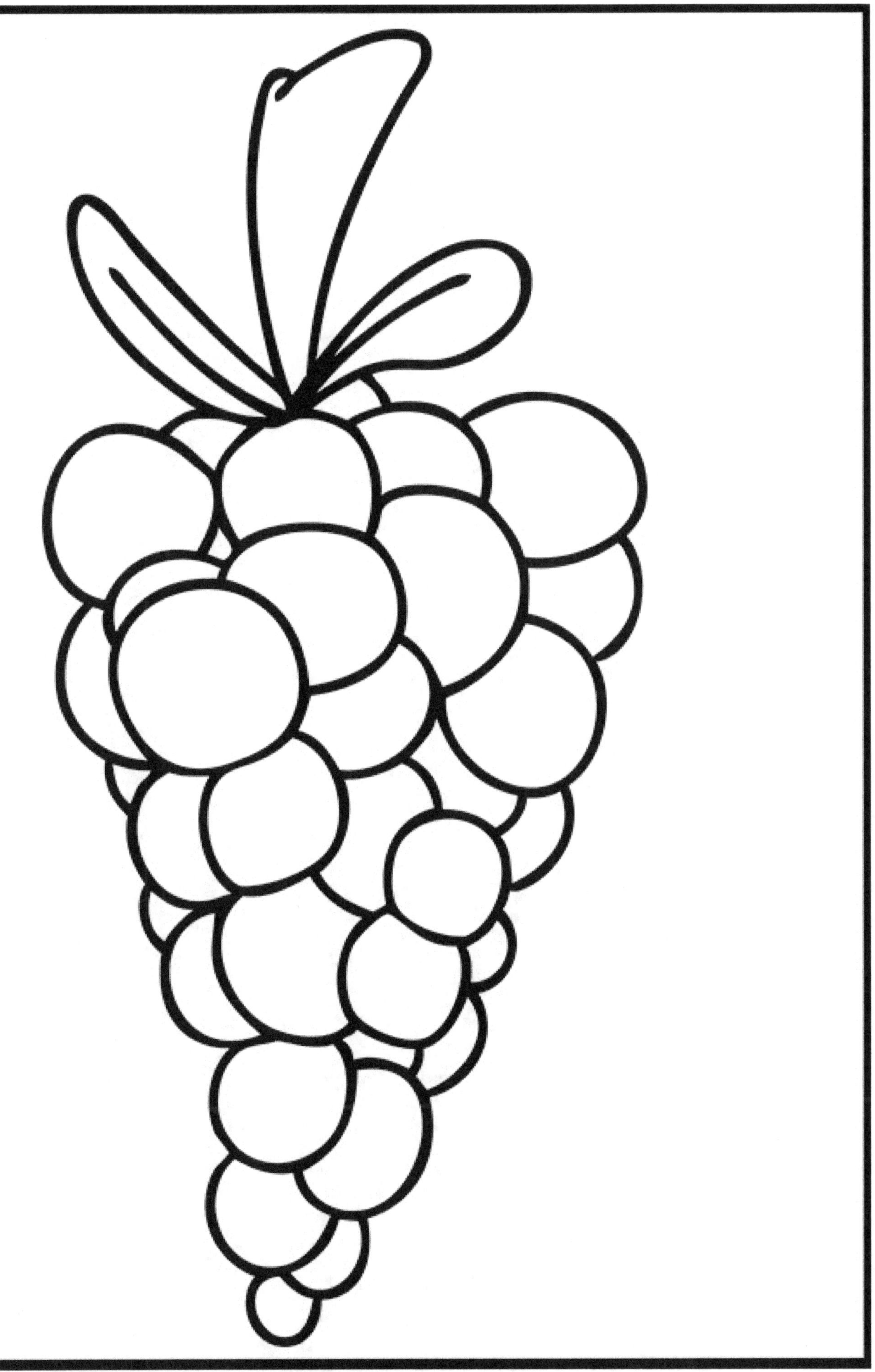

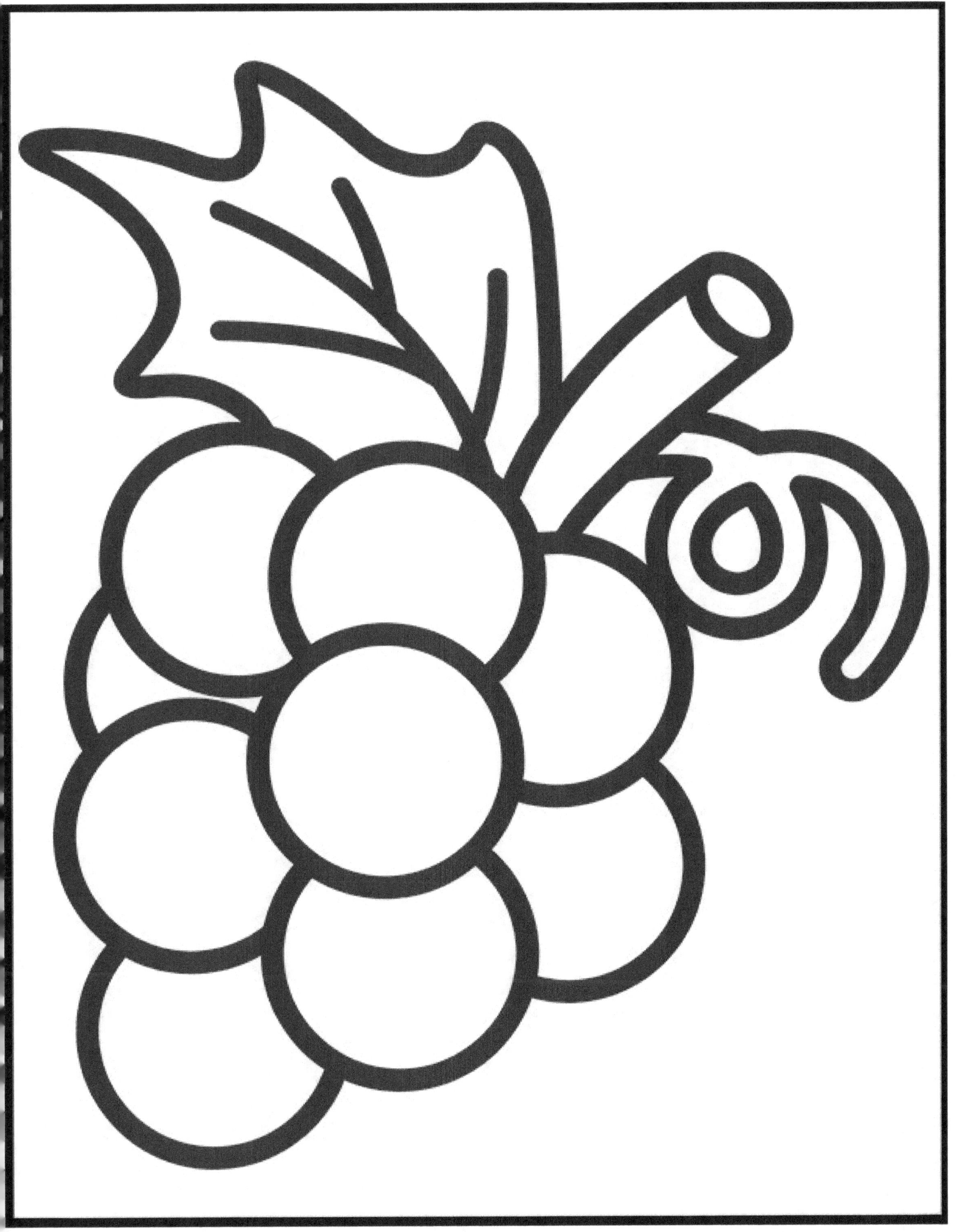

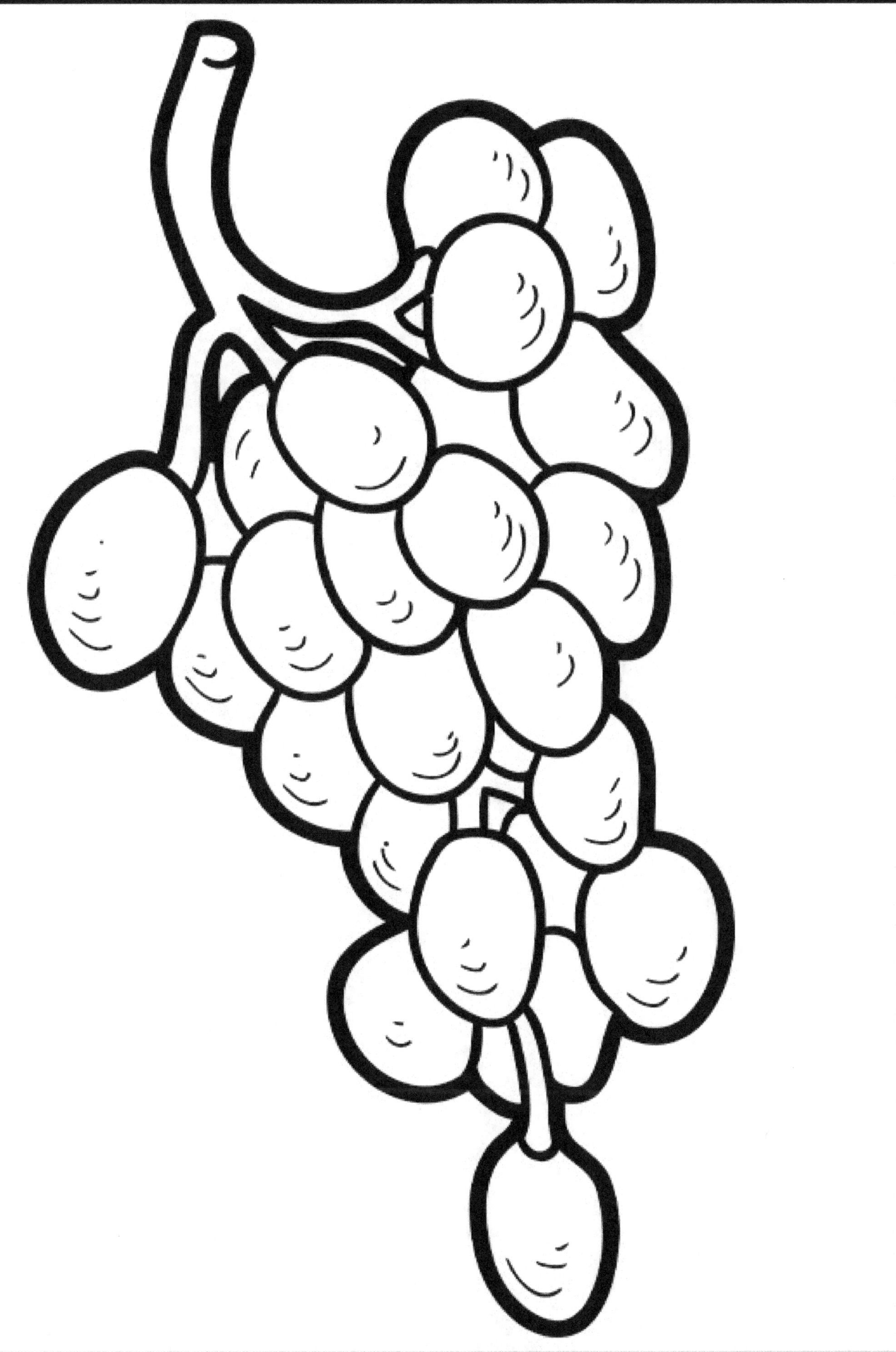

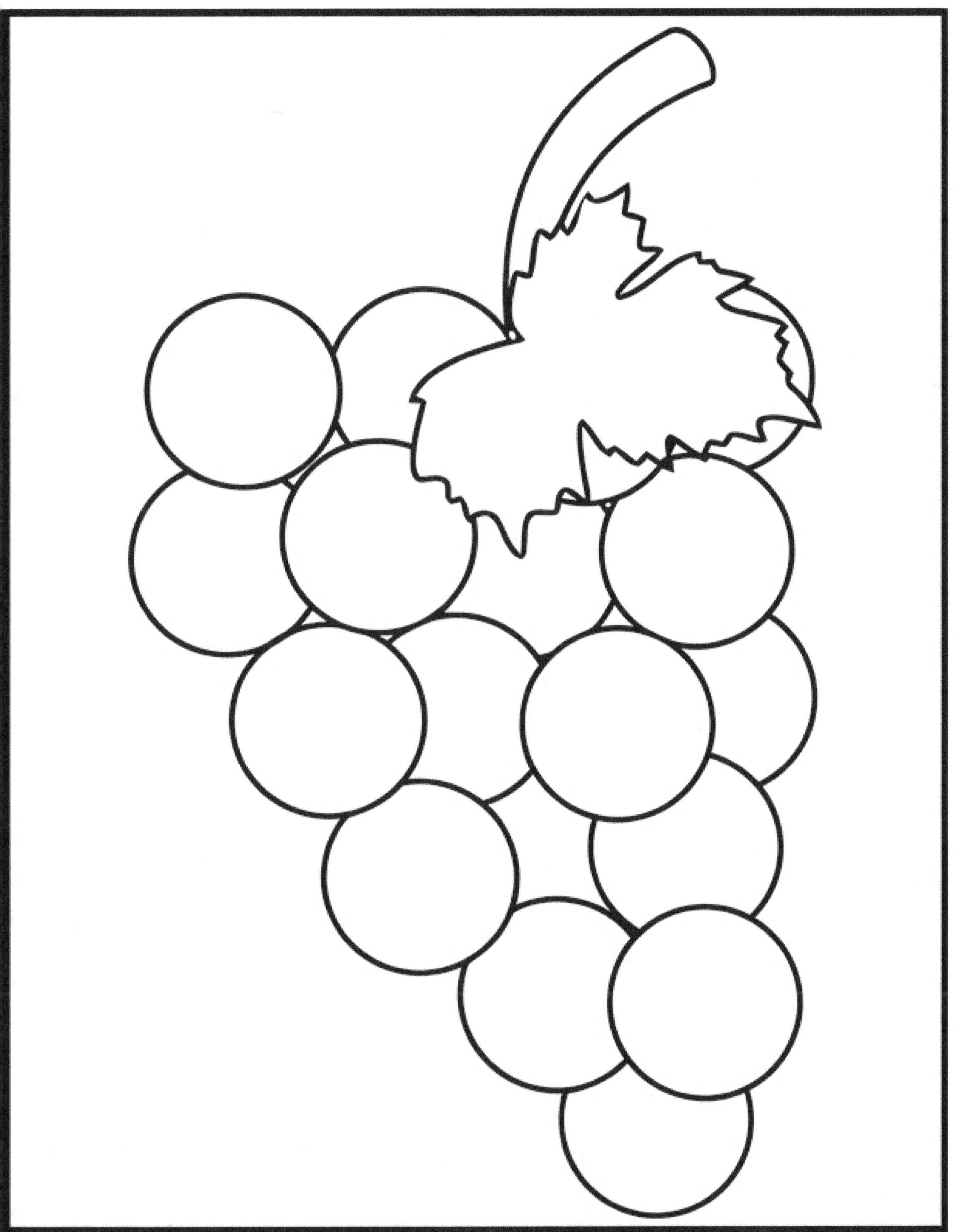

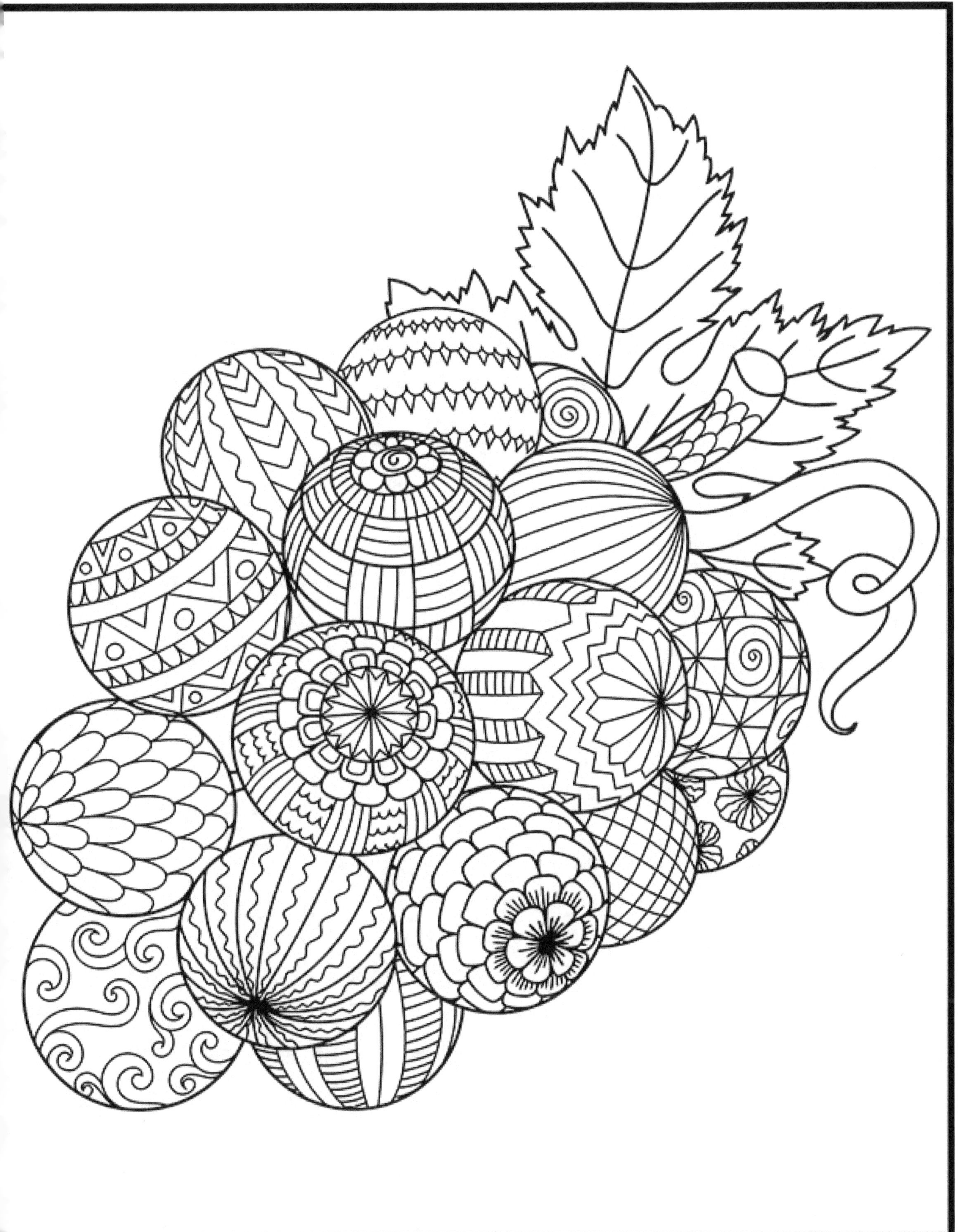

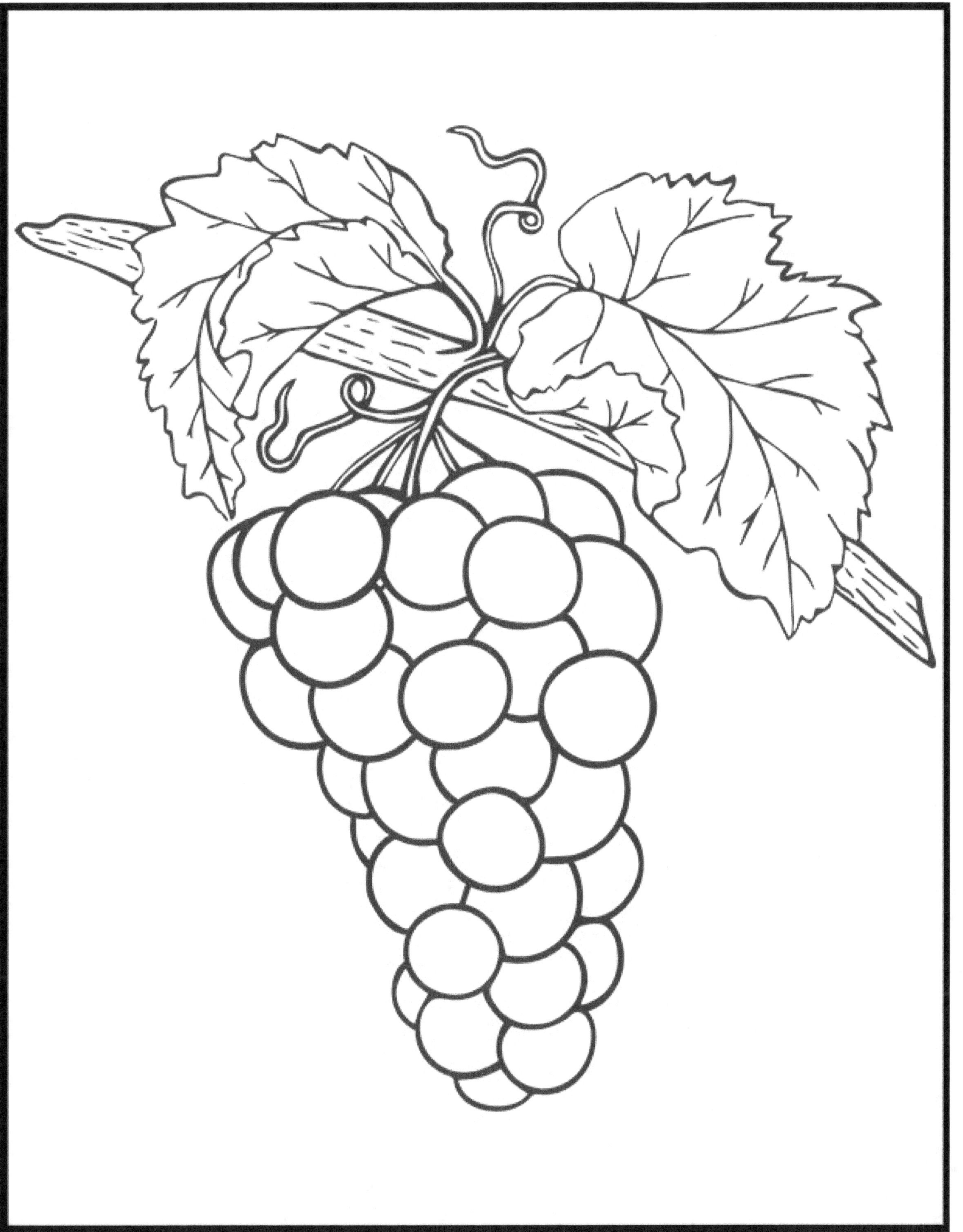

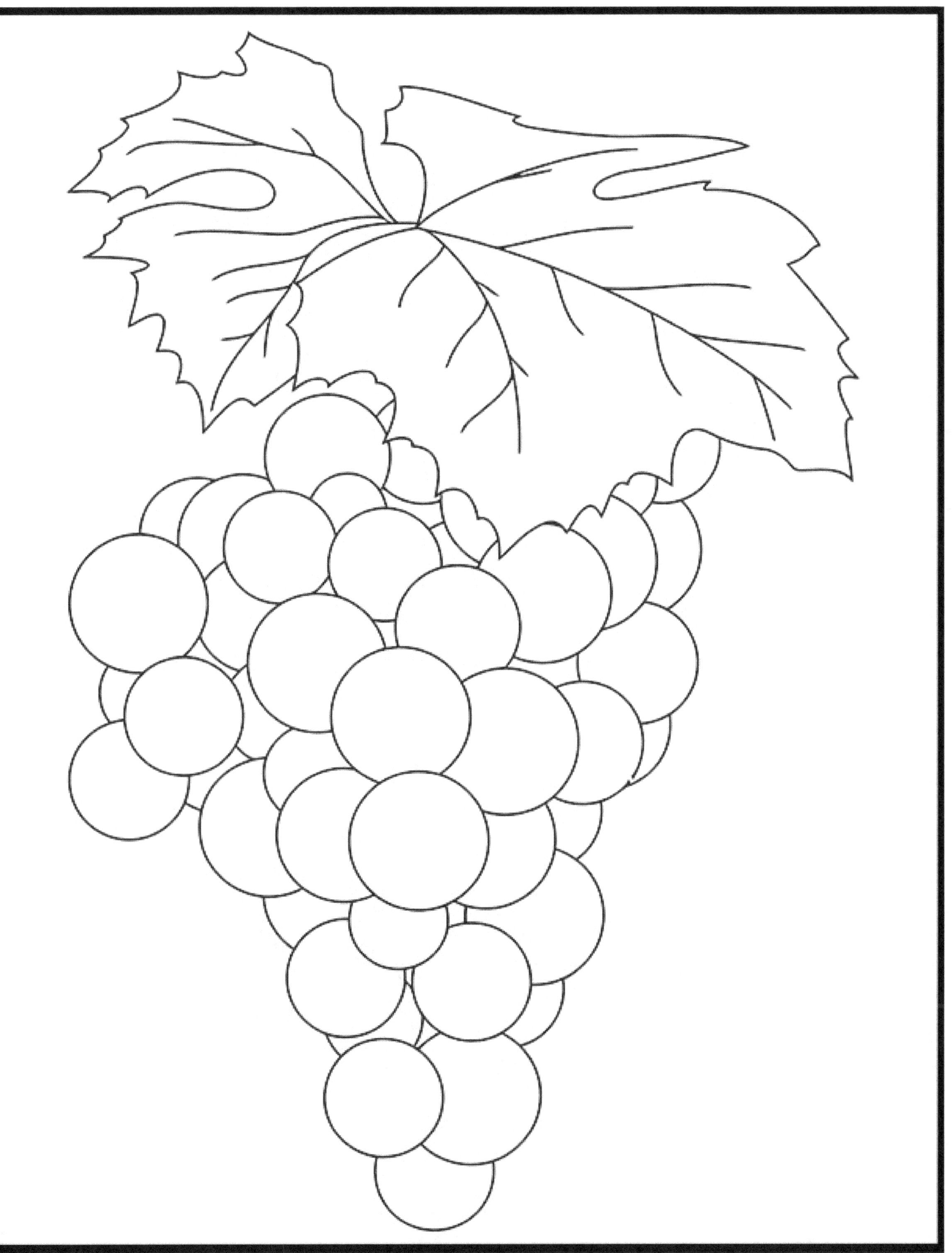

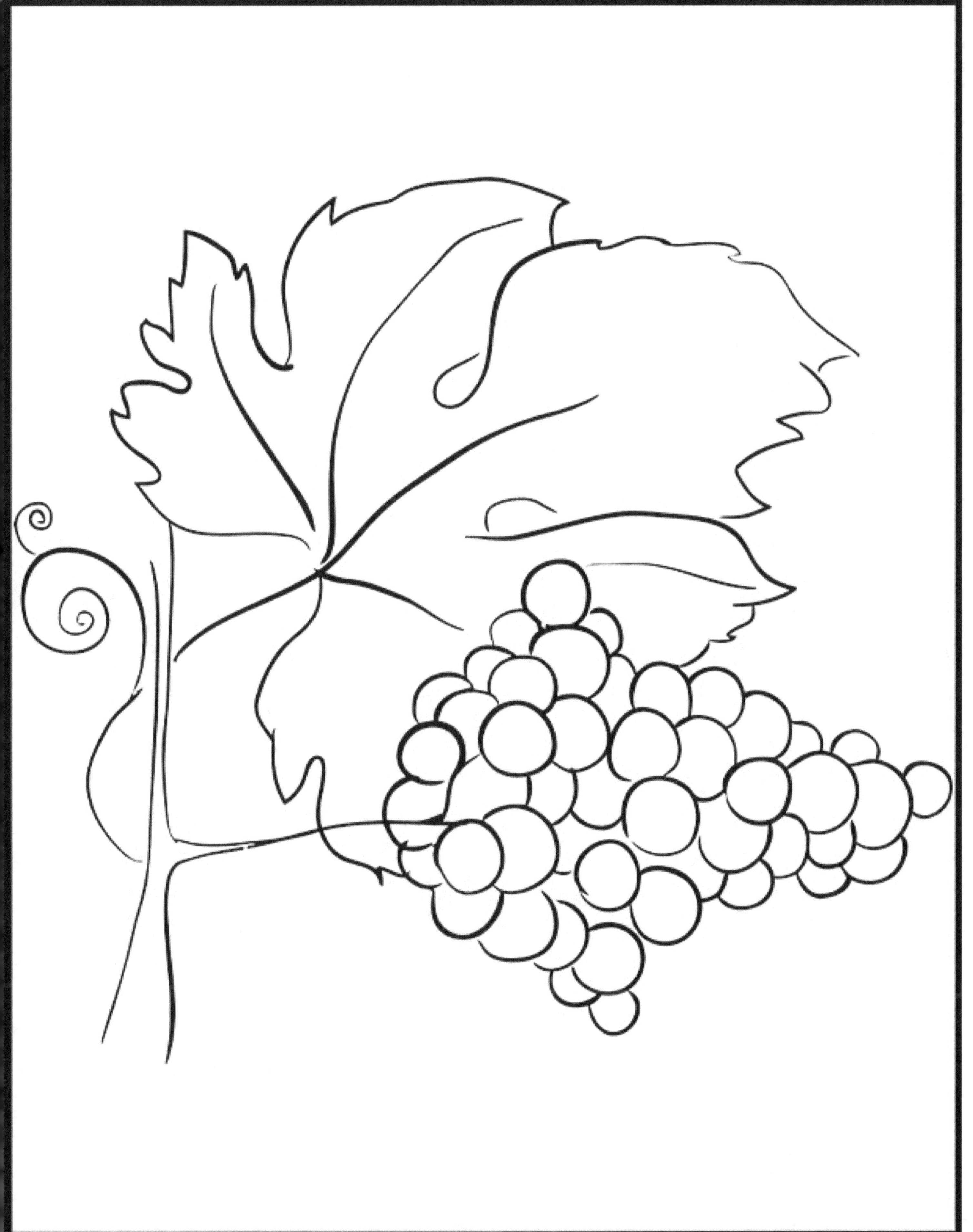

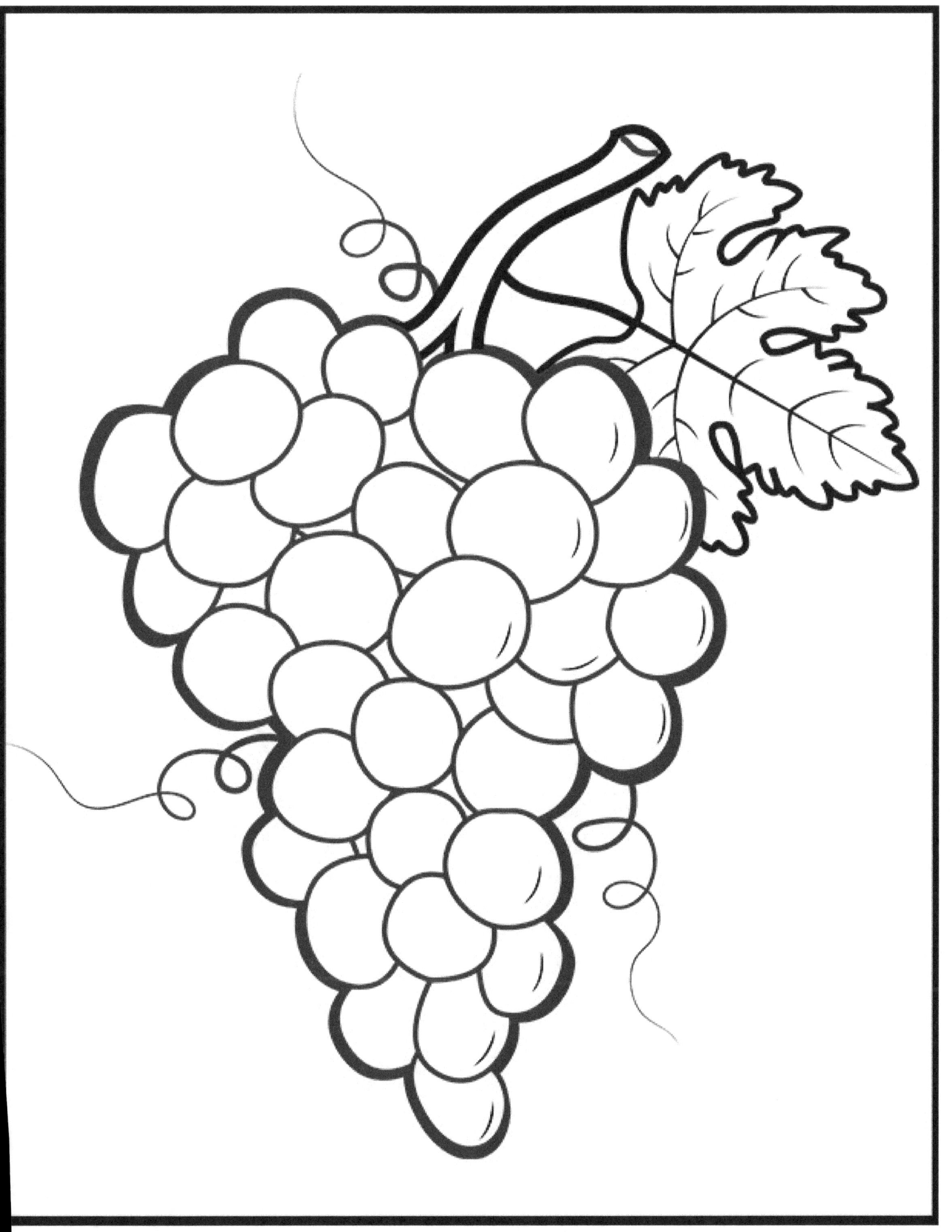

www.ingramcontent.com/pod-product-compliance
Lightning Source LLC
Chambersburg PA
CBHW082345270726
48658CB00017B/3139

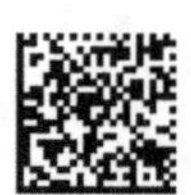

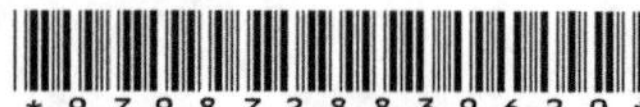